BEATEN

THE MONSTER WHO LOVED ME?

Peace and love for eternity. Everything is possible with God's grace.

love
D. Sarah

BEATEN

THE MONSTER WHO LOVED ME?

D. SAULS

To order additional copies of this book, contact:
Xlibris
844-714-8691
www.Xlibris.com
Orders@Xlibris.com
823123

CONTENTS

Acknowledgments vii

Chapter 1   So Young 1

Chapter 2   Mysteriosity 8

Chapter 3   High Demand 12

Chapter 4   Unexpected...28

Chapter 5   The Lies..39

Chapter 6   Deception 44

Chapter 7   Promises 49

Chapter 8   Bad Influence 56

Chapter 9   The First Audience 62

Chapter 10 Several Audiences to Follow...................................72

Chapter 11 First Hospital Visit..84

Chapter 12 Irreversible 95

Chapter 13 Scared Straight..120

Chapter 14 The Escape 134

ACKNOWLEDGMENTS

I WOULD LOVE TO thank my special cousin, the founder of "Moms Gotta Eat 2," for being the driving force in motivating me to tell my story and get this book done. Special thanks to my nieces and nephew for their love and support; my wonderful parents, I wouldn't be here without you; my father being the founder of An'n Rezone; my amazing other half; my twin sister who had been my biggest support team since day 1; the best bro-in-law in the world for helping me believe in human kindness; my brother for always giving the best advice without judgment and founder of CACTUS Center, LLC; my brother who shared his knowledge and helped my book cover come to life and founder of Entrepreneursfield Digital Marketing Agency.

Lastly, I would like to thank my friends who opened their doors when I needed it, offered a listening ear, and most importantly the ones who physically put themselves in harm's way to try and stop my abuser.

CHAPTER 1

SO YOUNG

WOULD YOU BELIEVE me if I told you I was the most insecure girl ever? If you knew me, you wouldn't believe it either. I remember growing up as a little girl, I was always being told how pretty I was. It was fairly odd for me because I never really saw what everybody else saw. It didn't matter because the majority of everyone—from adults and not just family members—would tell me. You would have thought with all this assurance of my beauty, I would have believed them, but I didn't. They say a person can be their worst critic. Well, that was me. I was that person. There was a reason I was so critical of myself. I didn't know it then being so young, but there was this deep dark hole in my heart. It was a sadness that existed that wouldn't go away. No matter where I was, it followed. No matter how happy I tried to be, it always found a way to take away my happiness.

It was so confusing to experience so much love and hate at the same time. I was born in Port-au-Prince, Haiti, and migrated to America at the age of four years old. There were two of us, me and my fraternal twin sister. You can tell we were sisters, but lots of people didn't believe we were twins. Coming to America was a dream for most immigrants, in hopes of a better life. I don't remember much about Haiti. Surprisingly enough, my sister and I have almost the same recollections of events. Whatever those recollections were of Haiti, I don't remember them being as bad as our experiences in America.

My mother and father already had family in America. My father went ahead of us, securing a stable job and his residency before bringing us over. Our first place of residence was in New York, where we stayed with my mother's sister and her family. It was a pretty fair introduction to America we (immigrants) so desperately wanted to be in. Our first day of school in New York wasn't too bad. We all know New York to be the melting pot of such a diverse group of people. When we were introduced to other children in Manhattan to be exact, it was fun and relaxing to be accepted. Just as we were starting to adapt to New York, it came to a screeching halt. Because of irreconcilable differences, our stay in Manhattan was short-lived.

The change happened so fast and unexpected that my father was forced to find a new place for us to live. He was able to find an apartment and a job in Newark, New Jersey. We lived in the hood of hood, where the drug dealers were feared and never reported. They owned the blocks, and you dare not to acknowledge that. If you ever wanted to know what hell looked like in '80s, just visit my life. It was definitely a drastic change, to say the least. There we were driving, and there it was bold as day. A big graffiti explicitly said, "Kill All the Haitians." We were definitely too young to understand the hatred and bigotry that lied in such powerful words. It's an unsettling feeling to be so young and have your heart drop to your stomach seeing that. Why do they want to kill all the Haitians? Isn't that where we are from? Mommy, Daddy, what does that mean? Why do they want us dead? Unfortunately, our parents weren't that knowledgeable to be able to explain this level of hatred as they were also being newly introduced to it. If we didn't know what it meant, then we were definitely about to be given a life lesson.

It was our first day of school in Newark, New Jersey. We had to be about six and going to kindergarten. As we entered the school, I remember my sister and me on opposite sides of the teacher as he introduced us to the class. The introduction was as followed: "Attention, class. I want to introduce you to the kids who just came from Haiti." I'm not sure why we couldn't be just introduced as the new kids and leave our nationality out, but needless to say, I wish he had. We were so scared being introduced into a whole new environment. I was hoping that we got to sit together and be able to support each other during this very difficult moment. Yes, of course, the first day of what was a foreign school to us was nerve-racking. Unfortunately, we didn't get to sit together and was separated in the class among the other kids. As the teacher explained, we needed to get familiar with the others. A couple of weeks went by, and it was surprisingly OK.

School had been dismissed, and we were waiting at the entrance of the door to be picked up by our mother like we normally did. This particular day, while waiting to be picked up, we saw a mob of children running after one boy. I want to say it was at least twenty to the one kid. We watched in fear as this one boy got stomped, kicked, dragged, and even beaten with a bat. This was unbelievable, and we couldn't understand why they were beating him so bad. What made it even worse was that no one was helping him. The poor boy just screamed and cried as they beat him endlessly. Of course, the teachers screamed for those hoodlums to stop, but what else could they do but call the cops and pray he wasn't beaten to death? The cops finally arrived, and you could watch as all those punks just disappeared so fast. I would say about one week later from that dreadful beatdown, my dad picked us up from school. As we were entering the hallway to our building, there he stood. Oh my goodness, I couldn't believe it. It was the young man who had got beaten up in front of our school. His eyes were bloodshot red, and that was the one that I could see. The other one was swollen shut, and there were so many cuts and bruises that stemmed from his face to his neck. It was so painful to look at him.

My father, who was a very talkative and nosy man, actually asked him what happened to him. To my surprise, as he told my father what happened, he began to cry. Would you believe that these pieces of human garbage beat this young man up because he was a Haitian? He told my father he didn't know any of them except one who went to his school. That was how they were able to identify that he was a Haitian. What kind of evil could exist in so many young men to nearly beat one person to death who looked just like them? Why was being from Haiti so bad? Why did they hate us so much? The poor kid was terrified to go to school. I don't remember what his outcome was, but I don't remember seeing him that much after that. I'm assuming his parents ran from such a dangerous environment and moved.

Just about one month into the school and we got a new student. This student was the plague who started the infestation of hatred toward us. You know children at such a young age are very easily influenced. Unfortunately, many tend to be followers and not leaders. Needless to say, once the kid found out we were from Haiti, we began to get teased a lot. It started with just the one little asshole and contaminated almost the whole class. The majority started to make fun of us and call us all kinds of names. This was the first time I learned what "HBO" was. It stood for Haitian Body Odor. Apparently, all Haitians smelled. It didn't matter that our mother always made sure we bathed, brushed our teeth, and wore clean clothes to school. We were told constantly that we smelled because of where we were from. I didn't even know Haitians ate beans out of a can and only came to America by boat. Unbeknownst to me because I don't remember eating beans out of a can. I could've sworn we actually got on a plane and flew to America. Hey, what did I know? Their ignorance was all they needed to ignore my reality.

We were so young experiencing so much hatred it started to feel like the norm. I thought it would be the end of it once we got to middle school. After all, it didn't start until that little asshole joined our class. Little did I know it was a hundred more of them in middle school. The older we became, the harsher the reality was. They were more violent and angrier, using very vulgar and explicit words. The first time I ever heard the word "pussy" was in middle school. I didn't even know what a pussy was and how it could stink. I heard countless vulgarities to say the least. Our parents shielded us from the dangerous world and didn't educate us on anything in regard to the outside world. We weren't allowed to have any friends, go to the library, talk on the phone, or even look out the window. All the things a normal childhood consisted of, we didn't have those. I always believed if we were able to go out and socialize just a little bit, then maybe they would see that not all Haitians were bad. Thankfully, our parents didn't see it that way because we could have ended up in very bad situations.

The older the kids got, the bolder they became. This was definitely bullying at its finest. Unfortunately, back then, there wasn't an outlet or a safe place you could go to report this. It seemed the teachers were just as scared of the bad kids as we were. It just seemed there was no end to it. I finally remember telling my father about it, and he told us that we had to fight back. "The reason they keep bothering you is because they think they can. Ignore them if you can, but if they touch you, fight back." My father said, "Girls like to do a lot of talking before they throw the first punch. Use that opportunity to size them up. See where you are going to attack first. They expect you to just talk with them or listen. You will do the opposite. If they have long hair, grab it and lock it in your hands. Get the upper hand, position your legs right behind theirs, and get them to the ground. Once you get them to the ground, don't stop punching until they cry for mercy." That would later turn out to be the best survival of the hood lesson he ever taught me.

It became an outright war it seemed. It was us against them. It seemed like all of them was against us until one day this young lady stood up for me. I was in class and undergoing the usual bullying, and she defended me. I couldn't believe it, she was one of them, and yet she was sticking up for me. She happened to be fairly popular and respected. This young lady turned out to be my best friend during those times. With her by my side, the bullying appeared to decrease. Unfortunately, she couldn't be everywhere I was, and I needed to protect myself and my other half (twin sister). We were of course getting older and my mom had just bought our baby brother into the world. Both our parents were working, but our mom had to work and take care of our brother. This led them to allow us to begin walking home alone. The walk wasn't long but maybe fifteen to twenty minutes tops, in which my best friend would walk home with us. Unfortunately, when she wasn't able to walk with us, it just seemed that much longer. My sister had made a friend also, and we all would walk home together. These kids were different; they didn't conform to the ignorance. They had their own mind and treated us like actual human beings. The bullies followed us home on occasion, and would you believe most of these bullies were boys? We ignored them as much as possible until that one moment when it couldn't be ignored. The only thing that made those walks less excruciating was knowing we were coming home to our cute baby brother to harass him with hugs and kisses.

It seemed like a different bully each time. I couldn't keep up with who hated us and who didn't. I just knew that I couldn't take it anymore.

I began to talk back and repeat the exact same things they would say to us. It began to shut them up a little, and then it escalated to that one girl trying to punk me. It started as the normal bullying session, the numerous threats of how I was going to get fucked up. I just remember my father telling me to stick up for myself. I told her to do it and then come fuck me up. My heart was racing, my stomach in knots, and I definitely felt like I was about to piss my pants. I just tried to remember my father's life lesson on if they touched me. There it was; exactly what my father said happened. It was as if he wrote the book himself. The girl got in my face and just kept talking. She didn't have much hair that I could maintain a firm grip. However, she did have enough where I could grab it and sideswipe her to get her to the ground. I followed every step and was able to get her to the ground. This rage took over, and I just began punching and punching until she had to beg me to stop. It was so bad they had to pull me off, and I still went for more, causing me to fall to the ground, bumping my head. I don't remember her getting one hit off, but there that big not stood on my head from the fall. My poor sister, who wasn't much for confrontation, just stood there in fear as she begged me to stop.

Trying to hide the knot from my mother, when we got home, I put a head scarf over my head. I went straight to bed and told my mother I wasn't feeling well. Anyone who has a Haitian parent knows that wasn't going to fly. I've never tied a head scarf covering my entire forehead, let alone not eat when I get home. My mother immediately told me to get out of the bed and removed the head scarf from my head. Countless screams followed as she was attempting to ask me what happened. As soon as I told her I was in a fight, there I was getting my behind beat by my mother with that hard buckle side of the belt. She didn't understand the gravity and importance of this fight. I needed to defend myself, but that went right over her head. I had no business fighting, and that was the only message she wanted to get across to me. I was devastated that I just got my behind beat for defending myself and completely terrified on what the next day would bring when I went back to school. I didn't know if there would be retaliation waiting or what.

To my surprise, the next day at school, kids were coming up to me, giving me pound and daps. They were even calling me Mike Tyson. One kid said, "Yo, I heard you whooped her ass." Kids were coming up to me that I didn't even know. It was even more shocking when the girl's cousins and friends came up to me. At first, I had my defense up, thinking they were going to try and jump me; they didn't. They literally told me that it was a good fight, and I got that off. Needless to say, the bullying stopped tremendously. I did get the occasional assholes who would try it no matter what. Even more disturbing was when boys would step up to me, but then I got the attention of this one really badass kid. He was feared by many, and nobody dared mess with him. He came up to me to say something about the fight and would occasionally have conversations with me. When most of those bullies saw me talking to him, they dared not approach me.

CHAPTER 2

MYSTERIOSITY

WHEN IT FINALLY seemed like it was coming to almost a halt, I couldn't help but wonder why all of a sudden. My father's words definitely held true. Bullies feed off fear; once you show them that you're not afraid and willing to stand up for yourself, most back down. I didn't really expect to come to such an abrupt but not complete end. I was definitely happy that I didn't have to fight as much. Yes, I was fighting a lot. Oh no, it wasn't just that girl. I even had to fight this little fat boy who was messing with my sister. I didn't mention that earlier because it really wasn't much of a fight. He was double my size and had double my punching power. It lasted for about a minute. I walked up to him and told him to leave my sister alone before I punched him in the face. Next thing I know, I was balled up on the floor in a fetal position, holding my stomach. He punched me so fast in my stomach I didn't even see it coming. However, it was the fight with the girl that gave us the respect we needed not to be harassed as much, at least I thought it was. I did have a couple of fights after that, but it became more so a jealousy thing. Stupid young girls trying to test the foreigner people were calling me Mike Tyson.

Remember the badass kid I told you about? Yes, the one who was talking to me more often, the one whom everyone seemed to admire, and had it not been for the fight, he wouldn't even know my name. I started seeing him after school a little more often than usual. I would often look for him in the hallways and classes but would never run into him. I didn't understand why he would be there after school but never in the school. Our conversations were limited, for I really didn't know what to say to a guy on a completely higher social level than me. We didn't have many friends as my parents were completely and ridiculously strict. I wanted to ask him why I never saw him in school but didn't even know how to ask him. I would never go and talk to him because he was always surrounded by all the popular kids. Even the major bullies at my school were showing him so much love. This boy was so mysterious it made me more curious to know more about him. I tried to become a little more alert when it came to this boy. I didn't see him every day but would see him quite often. I didn't even know his name.

We were now on recess and in the playground. Most of the games played were "Tag, You're It" and "Simon Says." Wow, that's going way back. I wonder how many can guess my age now just on those games alone, the days where the lady would sell the penny candies out of her house—Chic-O-Sticks, Now and Later, AirHeads, and more. Yes, I went all the way back. We didn't do much playing as my sister and I were very shy. Despite the fact they weren't bullying us as much, we still didn't fit in as much. Our finances were at poverty level. Our parents could just afford enough to put food on the table and clean clothes on our back. They did the best they could with the resources available to them at the time. Unfortunately for us, while the kids were wearing the New Balances, we had our fun steps purchased at Valley Fair. We had to hold on to those sneakers and take care of them as best as possible. When the Velcro strap started to wear out, tape was the best option for us to repair it. We didn't have the luxury of wearing Levi's and designer clothes. Most of the time, our clothes didn't even match. We had red pants with purple tops, and most of the time, we would wear the same clothes three times out of the week. It was hard for those kids not to notice and easy to exclude us from the fun and activities of the playground.

While left with nothing much to do, we were pretty much limited to people watching. I noticed that one of the gates in the playground had a big hole at the bottom of it. I also noticed kids going in and out of that gate during recess. I couldn't believe it and often wondered where they were going and if they would make it back in time before recess was over. As I was pondering, I looked toward the gate and saw Mr. Mysterious himself going under the gate into the playground. How interesting was it to see him coming into our playground during recess?

I was really confused and wondered why he was creeping under the gate to get into the playground. Why wasn't he already in the playground? Even more confusing was why it was so easy for them to come in and out of the playground with the teachers standing right there. It wasn't as if we weren't supervised. This was completely going over their heads. Were they really that blind, stupid, and oblivious that they couldn't see the new kids we had in the yard? He was never alone; he had several other young boys with him. I would say about at least four of them came into the playground that day.

The guys he was with began storming the playground, messing with some of the boys in the playground and flirting with some of the girls. He appeared to be a little more subdued as he just calmly walked the playground. He began walking toward me and my sister in the playground. I was getting extremely nervous and in disbelief that he was actually walking toward me. I started thinking of what I was going to say to him. As soon as I gathered my thoughts, he just said my name followed by a hello and walked right past me. I remember my sister surprisingly asked me how he knew my name and how I knew him. She was very alarmed as she was immediately able to see that he didn't go to our school. My sister was always four steps ahead of me. Although we were the same age, she always seemed to pick up things faster than me. As I mentioned earlier, he would talk to me, but it was always very brief. My sister never saw me talking to him. It wasn't as if I was hiding it or anything; it was just coincidental that she never saw us talking until that day he said hello to me in the playground. The questions that followed after that were endless. It was a good thing she did notice me talking to him because apparently, she had a little more insight than me. She knew that he didn't go to the school, apparently no school for that matter, and even knew his name.

Days to follow her insight of Mr. Mysterious would hold to be true. There we were sitting in the classroom, with the windows opened. The teacher was letting the cool breeze flow throughout the classroom. Interrupted by a burst of laughter from the entire class, I scanned the class to see what was so funny. Looking to the left outside the classroom window, he stood peeking through the windows, with his crew not too

D. SAULS

far away lurking through other windows. The teacher screamed at them to get away from the window. After several attempts and the class's laughter getting louder, they were not moving. I guess the attention made them want to be more defiant. The teacher raced toward the window in hopes of actually scaring them away from the window. That did seem to help as she forcefully closed the windows one by one, barely slamming their fingers. I have to say it was one of the funniest and entertaining things I'd seen in this school so far. It was uncontrollable laughter; the teacher had to tell us to stop laughing. She was pretty perplexed but amused at the same time. Even the teacher couldn't help but smirk at their blatant disregard for rules as they almost got their fingers slammed in the window.

This boy was so mysterious, funny, and bad. I found myself being really drawn to him. The saying holds true—"Good girls really do like bad boys." It was just something about him that I really wanted to know. Every time I laid eyes on him, I would get butterflies. I couldn't stop thinking about him and looked forward to seeing him each time. Little did I know he would later become the mysterious man I wish I never met, the terror that haunted my very soul and still haunts me to this very day. I should have known, but at that age, how could I know? The blatant disregard for authority and not conforming to the rules were red flags. I would later find out that those red flags would nearly cost me my life!

CHAPTER 3

HIGH DEMAND

IT WASN'T EASY being the children of such strict parents. In such a scary and horrid world, we needed to be educated on the realities of life. We had no real knowledge of sex, relationships, or the basic norms to deal with our peers. Our parents believed that shielding us from the world was protecting us, but it only caused us more harm than it did good. It left us vulnerable to the master manipulators of robbing one's innocence. As human beings, we're mostly always looking for attention and not really knowing the difference between good or bad attention. It's as if it becomes an adrenaline, and you just want it more and more. As time progressed, the older I became, and of course, I blossomed into a young lady. I was heading toward the age of puberty and got my period at the age of nine years old. Wanting so bad to get from my parents' tight grip, any little moment we could get to go outside, we would take it. We moved from the apartment building to literally a house right around the corner. At that time, we had to be about eleven years old going on twelve. It was one of those money pit houses, in which my dad was really good in construction and fixed it up to look pretty good. The corner stores were literally right across the street from our house. We even had the Chinese restaurant and candy store within our reach. We also had the local drug dealers within a short distance away. Their favorite hangout was usually the Chinese restaurant.

As I will continue to stress, we lived such a sheltered life. It was within years of living in the house that we knew that those guys who always hung on the street corners day and night were, in fact, dealers. We never got to hang out but would occasionally get asked to get Chinese food or cigarettes for my dad. We all remember back then that in the '80s and '90s, pretty much anyone could purchase cigarettes without any identification. It was there that lay all the danger, and sexual predatorial misconduct was at an all-time high. Every time we went to the Chinese restaurant, all the guys would talk to us. My sister and I were always told not to talk to the guys but never given the reasons not to. Those guys were really smooth talkers and aggressive. As soon as they saw us coming, it was as if we were the only females who existed at that time. All their energy would go into telling us how beautiful we were, constantly flattering us, and always asking for our numbers but, of course, never getting it. (We weren't even allowed to talk on the phone, so I don't see how that would have worked!) It's not like as soon as the food was ordered, we would get it right away. There was always a wait, which always ranged from ten to twenty minutes. Those guys didn't care how short or long the wait was; they exhausted every minute trying to run their game.

We were very young at that time, just barely turning twelve years old, and these were adult men. Their ages, from what I knew, ranged from twenty years old and above. They would ask us our age, so it wasn't as if they weren't aware that we were minors. It didn't stop them from trying to engage in inappropriate conversations. There were the few decent men who would always say, "Leave them alone. They are little girls," and oftentimes shield us from the vultures. We weren't let out the house much, but within a two-week time frame, we were there about three times. Some of the guys would grab us by our hands, some would talk sexual (I mean things that we didn't even know at the time what they meant), and some would even follow us home. Some would always ask if we were virgins and if they could pop our cherries. Oftentimes we would be so scared that our dad would be standing at the door as one of them attempted to walk us home. My dad had a really hot temper, and those guys didn't seem to have any respect or boundaries. I dreaded the day there would ever be an encounter between my dad and them.

I have to admit in the beginning, the attention felt good. We were advised not to talk to them and made all attempts not to. Unfortunately, it was really hard to ignore someone going out of their way to speak while ignoring the obvious of being ignored. It also didn't help that some of them were pretty funny and knew ways to get us to break our silence. I know I enjoyed the little bit of freedom we got being able to get out of the house and didn't want it to end. When I say we had no normal life as a child, it wasn't an exaggeration. We couldn't talk on the phone, couldn't have any friends come over, and God forbid if we watched TV pass a certain time. If it wasn't for going to school and the luxuries of having a window, I'm pretty sure we would have no idea what normal civilization looked like. The feeling of being desired, chased, and admired made me feel like we were in "high demand," never realizing that being in high demand to boys with no morals and education was never a good thing. What was really in high demand was those tight virgin jewels. We were young, lacked social skills, and lacked anything to do with street smarts. They were predators preying on us; the consistency and assertiveness wasn't a good thing. They were trying to bait our innocence and see if we would fall for it.

I'll never forget this one guy who loved to touch on me. He had no boundaries as to where he constantly grabbed my hands and touched my face and my waist. At such a very young age and with such strict parents, who do you tell? I never felt like I could talk to my parents because it always felt like we would be the blame for what happened. That little freedom meant so much to me; it felt like telling them the encounters with those men out there would take that away. Now realizing that wouldn't have been a bad thing. I always told him to stop and pulled away from him, but the more I pulled, the more aggressive he became. It now came to the point where I dreaded going to the store as I knew he would always be there. He wasn't stopping and appeared to make it his life's mission to harass me. I came to the realization that we were just going to tell our parents that we didn't want to go anymore. This bastard had the nerve to literally grab me and attempted to steal a kiss. As I cried and begged him to get off me, I heard a voice saying, "Yo, man, get the fuck away from her before I lay you the fuck out!" I turned around to see who was coming to my defense, and my heart dropped when I saw it was my crush, "Mr. Mysterious." The pervert just immediately walked away from me and apologized for bothering me. After that encounter with whom I now saw as my hero, the pervert never even looked my way.

Speechless, shaken, and numb to what just happened, it took a while for me to get any words out. When I finally did, I just thanked him and began to walk home pretty fast. As I was walking home, he began to chase me down with a bag in his hand. "You forgot your food!" he yelled. So shaken, I completely forgot about the food, and ironically this was one of the nights I went without my sister. I needed to wipe the tears from my eyes so my parents wouldn't notice anything. It was so sad that I was almost sexually assaulted, and I was thinking how I was going to keep it from my parents and my sister. He walked me close to the house and advised me to never come out of my house alone. He also dropped a bombshell and told me that guy whom he saved me from had served time for rape! I couldn't believe what he was telling me as my heart began to beat much faster. I asked him if he lived around here. The whole year that we lived there, I never saw him. He told me that he just came home, in which at the time I had no idea what that meant. So I asked, "What do you mean just came home? Did you just move here is that what that means?" He died with laughter as he explained that he just got out of jail. Of course, our conversation was cut very short as I didn't have much time and was out longer than usual. I didn't ask why he was in jail and didn't seem to really care. I was just so thankful that he came to my defense when he did.

Now that he was home, I began seeing him a lot. After that incident, I told my parents I didn't like going to the store with all those guys there. Unfortunately, I never gave any detailed reasoning as to why. They just said OK and left it at that. The only time I would see any of them was when we'd be walking home from school or peeping through the windows of our bedroom. He now became my obsession. I knew I was always intrigued by him and had a semi crush. After this encounter and him coming to my rescue, I had a full-blown crush. I would look forward to him running toward me and my sister every time he saw us come home from school just to say hello. He would always semi walk us home and skip away. I was learning a lot about him as I began to observe every little thing about him. I loved the way he walked and skipped when he was being playful. He always had a joke and appeared to make those around him laugh a lot. His sense of humor made him that much more appealing to me. He was always so respectful and always appeared to be looking out for us. I really wanted him to flirt with me and do all those things those other guys were doing, but he never did. He was one of the youngest on the block but still too old to be dealing with me according to the law.

I always felt that he was being respectful until that dreadful night. It was one of those nights when I looked forward to looking out the window to look for him. Seeing him up and down the streets a lot, I began to realize that he was in the same profession as all the other guys hanging on the street corner. It still didn't matter to me. Disappointingly, at that age, I didn't understand the gravity and disparagement that comes with this profession. I watched his every step as my eyes literally followed his every move. What else was left for me to do? We weren't allowed to even play in front of the house or sit on the porch. This was one of my forms of entertainment as the curfew for TV had already expired. There he was, just standing there and talking with some of the other guys. I watched in deep admiration until I see him standing still and leaning on a car. I see a young woman walking toward him, which was really nothing. Then she kept getting closer, closer, and closer to him. At any given moment, I was expecting him to move away from her. Unfortunately, that didn't happen. She got so close to him that their lips touched, and they began kissing.

My heart was crushed as I watched as my crush had someone else in his arms. I couldn't even go outside to intervene, nor did I even have the freedom to become a competition for her. Looking back at it, at such a young age, it was amazing that those children had so much freedom to do what they wanted. I mean, he was older than me, but even the kids my age were able to go outside and play. I don't remember ever seeing any parental supervision as they would be out all times of the night. I was very envious of what freedom they had and grew bitter toward my parents and the restriction they put on our lives. It wasn't fair were my constant thoughts. I wanted to be out there with him. I wanted to know what it felt like to be kissed by him. At such a young age, these weren't appropriate thoughts that any young lady should be having. I just knew how I felt and had no one to explain to me why they were wrong or right. I just knew that I felt them, and it appeared that I was never going to express them to him.

A couple of months went by, and he was still with that same girl locking lips. It appeared that this was something that I could definitely not come in between. I had no access to him other than those brief moments of me walking from school or him walking us to the front of the house. My attention and admiration for him began to dwindle as there were so many giving me so much more attention. Here it is that now I barely knew him, and I'd already fallen in love and heartbroken within the same breath. I caught the eyes of a full adult man, who was a distraction from Mr. Mysterious but became the thief of my innocence. I was definitely not age appropriate to be dealing with a man. I didn't have the mental capacity to understand a relationship, let alone sex. Yes, at twelve years of age, I was introduced to sex. All I remember was that I was young and completely clueless. The man was twenty-one years old, and he knew that I was a child but didn't care. Of course, he caught me on my way walking home from school and knew all the right words to say to manipulate a child. That was exactly what I was, a child! He would walk me home and began taking over the walks home. It was always a random guy trying to tag along on our walks home, but this guy began to dominate the walks. He was really good-looking and very muscular. In my eyes, he felt like a protector. But he was far from that.

We weren't able to talk on the phone, but he somehow convinced me to take his number. I told him that we weren't allowed to talk on the phone, but he taught me how to creep. He began watching the house and saw when my parents would leave. He was bold enough to come and knock on the door, asking me to come outside. The first time he did it, I was terrified but excited at the same time. My sister was so much stronger as she ignored them completely. When he came to the door, my sister was so upset as she insisted that I got rid of him. Once I realized that she wasn't having any of this foolishness, I tried to hide it as much as possible. Once he realized that she wasn't having him coming to the house bullshit, we began just talking on the phone.

He would tell me as soon as my parents left that I should call him. We talked for about one month until he asked me to become his girlfriend. Within that month, he continuously told me how much he loved me and bought me little gifts such as flowers and teddy bears that I would hide underneath my bed. Of course, at that age, you really think that means something. Exactly what it meant was that he was molding me to get me right where he wanted me. Talking on the phone wasn't enough for him, and he realized that he wouldn't be able to come to the house, so he was conjuring all ways that we could be alone together.

He began asking me if I could sneak out the house to come and see him as he lived literally up the street from where we lived. I was way too scared to do that as my parents were too observant. Although we were at the age where they could leave us home alone, they never left us alone at long periods. So he knew coming to my house was out of the question. He then convinced me to skip school and come to his house. He expressed how he really missed me and needed more time together. After all, I was his girlfriend and at least owed him to try. Sadly, that was what my young, naive mind had been led to believe. Everything he told me to do, I did it down to the tea. He was so good that I was able to skip school without any adults knowing I was gone. At minimum, the only moments we shared were kisses. Little did I know that horrible moment of me skipping school was going to be a lesson in sex that I could have waited to learn at an appropriate age. I remember hearing about dick and pussy at a young age but didn't understand the concept or how they came together. Well, apparently, today was going to be the day I learned.

Finally getting to sneak out of school, there he was waiting for me at the corner he told me to walk to. I was so excited as I was going to spend more time with my boyfriend. He told me we were going to get some ice cream and that he was going to take me shopping to get some new underwear. He wanted to see me in some sexy underwear and promised to buy them for me. Imagine the contrast of buying a twelve-year-old girl ice cream followed by sexy lingerie. Needless to say, we had to stop at his house first as he had to pick up something. He told me to make myself comfortable as he slowly searched for whatever it was us that took us to his house before getting my ice cream and going shopping. I sat at the kitchen table patiently and nervously waiting for him to be done so we could go. He gracefully led me to his bedroom, telling me to lie down as it would take longer than he expected. Whatever he told me to do, I always did it with no hesitation. He was always so kind and loving to me. I always wanted to make him happy. I felt safe, loved, and adored by him.

As I lay on the bed watching TV, he coincidentally joined me. He began to gently kiss me on the lips. This time it felt different as we both knew that it wouldn't be interrupted. We always had to sneak and kiss, and it always had to be really fast as our time together was always short. He pushed me down to the bed as the kiss became more and more passionate. Now it was escalating because he was touching me in places that he was never able to touch me before. He began taking off my shirt and training bra as he kissed my breast. Now my stomach was in knots as it felt good and bad at the same time. I really liked him, but I knew that this didn't feel right. I asked him when were we going to leave so we could go to our scheduled program. He told me that he wanted to spend time with me and didn't want to waste any of it getting ice cream. The harder he kissed me, the more I insisted on leaving. My breast was exposed, and he began going down to my sacred jewels. He put his hands down there and slowly tried to take off my underwear. I begged him to stop as I pulled them back up. At this given moment, I knew that I have bitten more than I could chew. I began to cry as he pulled his dick out, and it was hard, something that I'd never seen before. I had no idea what to do with it. I just knew that I didn't want it.

He grabbed my hands and put it on his very hard part. At this point, I was crying and wanted to go home. I asked him to stop and told him that I didn't want to do this, that I just enjoyed kissing him. He began to get upset and nervous at the same time. He begged me to stop crying and began to console me. He told me he was so sorry and really loved me. It really felt like he was feeling bad for what he was doing and had a conscience. I cried myself to sleep as I lay on his chest. Finally, that nightmare was over, at least I thought. It was early in the morning, and we had all the way until school got out in the afternoon to spend time together. He let me sleep for a couple of hours as he began to wake me up with kisses. I kissed him back and asked him if we could finally leave now. He began to kiss me hard again as he recycled the same behavior. I began crying again, but this time he became annoyed. He told me to stop it and behave like his girlfriend. He told me that was what girlfriends did for their boyfriends. He pulled it out again and quickly took my panties off. He pushed me to the bed and quickly pushed himself inside me. I was a virgin, and him inserting himself inside me was every bit of painful. I cried as loud as I could, but that didn't stop him. It appeared to arouse him even more as he began to make noises that were louder than my cries. He covered my mouth with his hands as his noises began to overpower my cries. Finally, he stopped, and it began to feel like I had peed on myself, later learning that he had ejaculated in me.

I felt disgusted as my cries never stopped, and my nos went ignored. After he finished with me, he was now realizing that he was going to have to get rid of me soon. My cries were inconsolable at this time, and he needed to do something to get me to stop. He kissed and rocked me until my cries subsided. He continued to convince me that this was what boyfriends and girlfriends do. "This was a very private moment, and no one can know about this. If your parents find out, they wouldn't understand, and I would never be able to see you again" was what he told me. "You could barely see me now, so why would it matter?" He laughed off my comment and led me to the bathroom and began to bath me. He scrubbed my body from head to toe as he inserted his fingers into my jewels and thoroughly cleaned it out. After getting rid of all the evidence, he told me to get dressed. Now we were finally going to get my ice cream. At this point, I just wanted to go home and wished this day never happened. I never wanted to see him again and was so mad at myself that I cut school. I was even mad that no one ever noticed that I was gone to even stop this from happening in the beginning. We got the ice cream, but I barely had any appetite for it. I had stopped crying, but I was really sad and didn't really fully understand what had just happened. He walked me back to the school, with enough time for me to fall in with all the other kids as school was dismissed. My sister and

I didn't have any classes together, so she only realized that I wasn't at recess. I told her that I wasn't feeling well and stayed in the nurse's office during the time of recess. How could she know that I was lying to her?

As we walked home, I dreaded seeing him on the street corner that led to our house. I no longer had those bubbly feelings for him and wanted nothing to do with him. I told no one what happened, not even my sister. I just wanted to erase that moment and feeling from my body. I didn't understand that I had just been robbed of my innocence by the man who claimed to love me. There was no outlet or explanation as to "good touch, bad touch" like they have now. You know I wasn't going to tell my parents, so I was left to keep this secret to myself. This man was a "monster." Despite violating me, he continued to tell me he loved me. We turned that dreadful corner, and there he stood, eagerly awaiting my arrival. I kept my head down as we turned the corner and completely acted like I didn't see him. He began to scream my name as I urged my sister to walk faster. My sister was very intuitive and wanted to know why he was so aggressively calling my name. I just urged her to walk faster as he tried to approach us. This dreadful day had come to an end in which it was now bedtime. As I was getting ready to fall asleep, I heard loud noises. The noises appeared to be really close to my window. Deciding to take a peek out the window, there he stood right across the street from our house, staring into it. I quickly closed the curtains and prayed that he didn't call my name or have the urge to ring our doorbell. That night I was mixed with so many emotions of loving him and hating him at the same time. He spent the entire night staring into our house as I secretly watched him, not being able to get any sleep myself.

I was in so much pain and didn't know how to make it go away. My entire body was hurting from his constant grabs as I tried to fight him off. My jewels were in complete duress, feeling like they had been ripped open as he was very well endowed. My heart was once again broken as I felt so betrayed by him. I really believed he loved me and wanted to keep me from harm. Never would I imagine that he would be the one to inflict the most hurtful pain I've yet to experience in my life. Sleepless with no appetite or desire to get out of the house, I had to fight. I tried to fight the sickness I felt in my stomach and heart, but it was overpowering. I begged my parents to let me stay home. I was sick to my stomach and didn't want to risk the chance of running into him on our walk home. Thankfully, it was now a Friday, and my parents agreed to letting me stay home. This meant that I didn't have to see him until Monday. I didn't call him, and that made him completely anxious. It was as if in his mind, I was really his girlfriend. He pursued me as a girlfriend who was just momentarily mad at him and would stop at nothing to get my attention. I knew his voice and was hearing it more than I wanted to.

It was now Saturday, and my parents were getting ready to step out for a long while. As they were leaving, I actually asked if my sister and I could go with them, in which they declined. As soon as their car pulled off, not even ten minutes passed by and our doorbell was ringing. My heart dropped to my stomach as I knew it was him. I hated him for having the balls to even come to my door after what happened. I tried to ignore it as long as possible, but he wasn't letting up. My sister encouraged me to hurry up and answer it so I could quickly get rid of him before our parents returned. I stormed to the door in a fit of rage, having all intentions of cursing him out. As I opened the door, there he stood with a rose and a teddy bear. It sidetracked me for a little, I'm not going to lie, but I quickly went back on track. I asked him not to ring my doorbell, thanked him for the bear, and asked him to please leave me alone. He told me that if I didn't call him or stop ignoring him, he would have no choice but to come to my door. He insisted on not leaving until I committed to calling him. Completely fearful of my parents returning and seeing him standing at the door, I said what he wanted to hear so he could leave.

I resumed calling him, but my feeling was completely different. The very sight of him made me sick, but I didn't know how to shake him. He insisted on seeing me alone again, and I knew for a fact this wasn't going to happen. I knew in my heart that he wasn't going to be able to manipulate me into cutting school again. I called, but the calls were less than usual. He noticed a change in the efforts of calling him. I tried to tell him that my parents were starting to get a little suspecting of me using the phone when they weren't home or asleep. He wasn't buying it, and each time the phone call lessened, he was at my house, making his presence known. It was getting to a point where I didn't care, and I felt like I wasn't going to let him intimidate me anymore. I began to just ignore him completely and even the screams outside our house. Eventually, I thought he would just get tired of being ignored and move on. Apparently being ignored made him more agitated and crazier. One week went by, and I didn't hear from him or see him outside on our walks from school. I was excited and felt relieved at the same time. It was finally over!

Despite the fact it appeared to be over, my parents began to sense something was off with me. I was a little bit drawn back more than usual, and my mood had drastically changed. I was a really good student and would mostly do my homework on time. Since the day I skipped school and was given a drastic crash course on sex, my focus was off. I wasn't completing my homework on time, and my grades became drastically dropping. My parents, already being insufferable, became worse. As if you can imagine, there could be any higher level than that. I was just really happy that he finally was leaving me alone. The week was coming to an end as we were approaching the weekend. My parents were asking me what was wrong and aggressively seeking a response. There was no way they were going to get anything out of me, so I continued to tell them that I was fine. We were now well into Sunday, and everyone was getting ready for bed early to get ready for the week. Annoyed by the extra attention my parents were giving me, I tried to get ready before them. I just wanted to be left alone. Everyone had finally gone to bed, and I heard this horrible fucking voice. Yes, would you believe his horrible voice? This time instead of being across the street, he was directly in front of the house. He was not talking in codes now; he was screaming out my name. This man had completely lost his mind! I pulled the curtain back and waved him away. He fearlessly told me he was not leaving until I came and talked to him. I guess he forgot my age and the strictness of my parents, so I was just going to ignore him again until he went away.

Oh no, the doorbell had just rung. It's about 11:00 p.m. now, and I know my parents were fast asleep. I looked out the window, and it was him ringing the doorbell. I hastily but quietly ran down the stairs to get to the door. I was in complete fear as I opened the door and asked him if he was fucking serious. He sarcastically told me, "I told you what would happen if you ignored me or stop calling." He was talking really loudly, and I was now at this point of begging him to leave in fear he would wake my parents. He insisted that he wasn't leaving and pushed his way through the door into the house. I nearly shit my underwear in disbelief that he had become so bold and behaved as if I lived alone with no parents. I quickly locked the door and pulled him to the back of the house. We had a room in the back leading to the backyard. I figured if I took him back there, he would be able to quietly say his peace and leave. It was pretty dark, and I also figured even if my parents came down, I would hear them, and we could just keep quiet until they went back to sleep. My heart began to pound as I began to hear footsteps coming down the stairs within ten minutes of his arrival. We slid to the floor and lay down until whoever had come down left. I saw the lights turn on and heard footsteps, but it was not like they had come down to get something to drink or eat. It seemed they had heard something and were searching for where the noise was coming from. We crawled to the corner of the back room to hide as best as possible, hoping that once whoever it was turned on the light and saw no one there, they would immediately give up and go back upstairs.

I looked toward him as we both were trying so hard to stay quiet and saw this fear that I never knew existed in him. He was terrified of getting caught. I wondered if he was such a coward, why would he even take the chance of coming to my house to begin with? The footsteps were getting closer and closer to the door. The knob began to turn, and the light flicked on for the back room that we were in. The door swung open, and I saw my dad angrily walking directly toward us as it was very hard to hide now. As my dad was walking toward us, trying to make out who he was as his baseball cap was down low, the coward jumped, stormed past my dad, rapidly opened the door, and literally leaped off the back room porch. I've never seen anyone move so fast aside from the Olympics. He bolted like Usain Bolt would while jumping hurdles. It all happened so fast, and he wasted no time just leaving me behind. I literally just saw his dust as he bolted out of the house. I only let him in because I wanted him to leave me alone and the noises to end. It appeared that this was all that needed to happen for him to actually leave me alone. Now I was left to deal with the angry wrath of my father.

I was at a loss for words as my father was screaming at me, asking me who the hell that was. He ran back upstairs infuriated as he went to get my mother. I already knew what my fate was going to be. I just hoped that if they killed me, it would be a fast death! I was downstairs in complete fear, contemplating if I should run out the door also. At that time, it felt like anything would be better than meeting my fate in the hands of my parents. Finally, they both were downstairs, screaming, yelling, kicking, hairpulling, dragging, and interrogating. No matter what, I was determined that I wasn't going to say a thing. They asked me if I was having sex with him and how old he was. I answered no questions as it defeated the purpose in my eyes. Why would I incriminate myself even more? I was already in trouble, and nothing I could say would change that. As they interrogated me for hours and saw that I wasn't cracking, they went and dragged my poor sister downstairs and began to interrogate her. My sister knew mostly what I was doing but not everything. I tried to hide a lot from her because she didn't approve of my behavior. She always tried to talk me out of every bad idea, but I never listened. I always felt so caged and wanted to break free, while she was so much stronger than me, handling everything like a trooper. It pained me to watch as they began whipping her for answers, but she never told on me. Unfortunately, my parents never trusted us to begin with. Well, this made matters even worse! It was pretty devastating as the interrogation never stopped until the following morning. They were already noticing a change in my behavior; this exasperated their inquiries. At this time, I was exhausted, injured, and sleep deprived. School hours were approaching, and my parents were debating if I should go to school or not.

Me not going to school would mean that one of them would have to miss work. My father being the bigger breadwinner, it was decided that it would be my mother to stay home. I felt horrible. My lip was busted, I had gashes on my head, and there were nail marks from them trying to choke the truth out of me. I had put them in a very bad position where they didn't have time to think and reacted out of anger. I never faulted my parents for that ass beating. I just hated that my sister got one that she didn't deserve. A couple of days went by, and the bruises were starting to fade away. I was allowed to go to school, but my parents never once said not to tell anyone what happened. When I got to school, even though the bruises had faded, you could still see them. Of course, the teachers began asking what happened, in which I told them I had gotten into a fight with one of my peers. I would have hated for anyone to have to get involved, so I felt it best to keep it quiet, sooner learning that anything done in the dark would come to light. It was painful to face the reality of the drama I had brought into our home. I was ashamed of myself and angry that I was so easily manipulated.

A couple of weeks went by, and I began feeling sick and nauseous. My parents asked me every single day since catching the boy in the house if I was sexually active—a question that no matter how many times they asked it, I exercised my right to remain silent. As my mood began to change, my period was late, and my appetite was increasing, my mother knew right away that something wasn't right. She tried using a different approach and actually tried talking instead of yelling to get me to admit my indiscretions. It didn't work. She told me she believed that I was pregnant, and the only way that happened was if I was having sex. She looked at me with disgust as she told me that if I were, she would be sending me away. At this point, I really didn't care; it already felt like my life was over. They now began insisting on me telling them who the boy was at the house. Ironically, since that incident and he bolted out of the house, I never saw him again. My dad didn't get too much of a good look because as soon as the lights went on, he wasted no time making his escape. I felt that telling them who he was would only make matters worse. I'd already caused enough trouble as it was. I was warned that one way or another, the truth was going to come out.

We got home from school the following day, and both my parents were surprisingly home. I was told to eat and shower really quick because

I had a doctor's appointment. Of course, now my heart was at the pit of my stomach, knowing the truth was going to come to light. It was later confirmed that I indeed was pregnant. No discussion to follow after, and the next couple of days, I was in another hospital room. Hours later, I was no longer pregnant. The tension in the house was unbearable as my parents barely talked to me. My mother tried to convince me to go live with my aunt in New York, in which I actually considered. The thought of leaving my sister outweighed that thought process. Things were never the same as I was always reminded of shaming the family.

My mother began talking to one of her sisters, who advised her to just get me into some after-school programs or let me get a job. She suggested that a job or sport would help positively distract us. Thankfully, my parents took that advise, and I got my first job. Getting ready to now start high school, it would have been harder for them to restrict us as much. Things were definitely different, and I overheard my parents talking about moving away from the block we lived on. My parents were always in fear of me running into that guy again and possibly resuming where we left off, never knowing that I wanted to leave as much as they did. I welcomed the fresh start and wanted a change of view. Surprisingly, after the incident of him leaving the house, I never saw him again. It was as if he never existed and was a figment of my imagination. My parents did decide to relocate as we started our new journey to high school. I have to admit, I oftentimes wondered what happened to him but was so thankful I never had to see him again.

CHAPTER 4

UNEXPECTED

ALL PACKED AND ready to go, it was nothing but excitement flowing through my body. I dreaded living in the hood, where boundaries and morals were nonexistent. It felt good knowing that I wouldn't have to see those perverted men ever in life. Although I never saw the one who took my innocence, I always imagined one day that I would run into him. I don't know where he disappeared to, but I knew it was only a matter of time before I would probably see him again. It was hard to avoid any of those thirsty guys because they were literally on our path to get to our house. I was looking forward to not having to deal with that, let alone all the bullies we dealt with at that school. It felt like it was going to be a fresh start with new beginnings. All those dreadful memories in the old house, I planned on working hard to rid them from my thoughts. We were going to an entire new school in a completely different neighborhood. Highschool, here we come! What a difference a different zip code could make. Looking at the beautiful trees and the quiet neighborhood, it was already seemingly peaceful. There were no corner stores with a bunch of hoodlums hanging around. This felt good for a change, not having to come up with ways to avoid those aggressive men. Not having to dodge through a group of thirsty men just to get home.

My life was seemingly back on track. I was in high school around new people who appeared to be fairly decent. I was able to get a job and change up our wardrobe just a little. The kids were way less cruel; I'm assuming being a little older played a major part in it. I was feeling pretty broken with having to deal with such a traumatic experience. I needed to be around people who didn't make my life any worse. You never know what people are going through and should at best treat them how you want to be treated. It was starting to feel like we somewhat had a normal life. Although my parents were still pretty strict, we always knew it was how they saw fit to protect us. I was starting to feel less suffocated and was even able to join track in school. It really helped build my moral and actually made some friends. As time progressed, my parents became a little more lenient with having a bit of a social life. Working and playing sports was a great distraction for me. We were even able to go to the movies as long as our school grades were good.

My sister and I were very well liked in high school. Our freshman year, we met this beautiful young lady, who happened to be a senior. She was the most beautiful and well-dressed senior in that high school, at least in my eyes. She was very popular and happened to have a beautiful voice. She amazingly had a singing group, in which the high school we went to were for children of many different talents. She found out we were Haitian and literally took us under her wings. She would wait for us after school at times and give us a ride home. She was like a guardian angel and made going to school that much easier. It was a big difference from going to a school that bullied us for being Haitian to now finally going to one who accepted us for just that.

The guys were definitely a different speed and age appropriate. There were a lot of guys with crushes, but they weren't aggressive and actually understood what "no" meant. I had my fair share of kisses and make-out sessions but never fully had the desire for an actual boyfriend. I didn't trust men but found myself paying attention to all the older guys. There were so many good ones who were after me, but I always seemed to choose the bad ones. Although our lives appeared to be much better than before, I found myself revisiting that dreadful moment when I skipped school. Surprisingly, I was doing very well in school, but it did help to have one of the smartest sisters in the world. She was always so studious and always tried to encourage me to do better in school. Getting through high school was pretty fun. I made a lot of friends and enjoyed getting to know their amazing talents. I loved working and making extra money to buy clothes, shoes, pizza, and Burger King for my sister and me. You know the luxuries of being youthful. My sophomore year in high school, I was able to get a second job while my sister got her first job. During that time, our mother started encouraging us to save our money. At fourteen years old, I proudly opened up my first bank account. Time is moving so fast as high school was coming to such an abrupt end.

Now approaching the end of my senior year of high school, we were starting to make plans for college. Pretty excited for the future, I was deciding on which colleges to go to. We were working hard and trying to save as much money as possible. We caught the bus back and forth to school, work, and home. One day, while catching the bus from work, standing at the bus stop, we saw what appeared to be a familiar face. I tried not to stare, but that face just looked oh so familiar. It seemed that we probably looked familiar to him also as he continuously stared at us. He had a hat on, so it was kind of hard for me or my sister to make out exactly who he was. We both did agree that he looked familiar. As we reached our final stop, we were coming off the bus and noticed that he was coming off the bus also. As soon as we came off the bus and at proximity to each other, we all immediately realized who each other was. My heart dropped to my stomach, and butterflies began to develop in my stomach. I couldn't believe that he was right there in front of me, at such proximity. I never expected that I would see him again as it was so unexpected. I was extremely excited that I had way more freedom than when I last saw him. That dreadful night looking out my window watching him lock lips with my competition, that really wasn't a competition. I mean, how could I compete when I couldn't even go outside? Yes, guys, it was Mr. Mysterious, and he was just as happy to see us as we were to see him. He was always so funny when we were younger; he appeared to still have that same sense of humor.

We began walking home as he walked in our same direction. Still in shock that we actually ran into each other, we asked him what he was doing around here. Surprisingly, he lived right up the street from our new house. What was the likelihood that he would move to live up the street from us again? It was almost too good to be true, almost like it was meant to be. The most ironic thing was that he literally moved a couple of months after we moved. We exchanged lots of laughs on the walk home and even exchanged numbers. I knew that I looked forward to the moment of being able to talk to him and actually spend time together. At this present moment, I was preoccupied with finishing up school and graduating on time. I didn't call him right away but thought of him every step of the way. Nearing the end of graduation and on the right track, I finally saw the light. One month had passed since our encounter at the bus stop, and I had all intentions of calling him. It looked like he got tired of waiting and beat me to the punch. He didn't have my number, but he did remember where I worked at as I mentioned to him on our last encounter. What a smile it bought to my face as I saw him walking toward me with a big smile on his face. He asked if I lost his number and asked why I never called. I explained to him where my focus lay but did assure him that I would give him a call soon. He assured me that he would patiently be waiting and told me he looked forward to my call.

The feelings that I had for him was very overpowering as he was exciting, funny, and handsome. Just the thought of getting to know him was exciting to me. Well, the faith of my graduation was secure, and I had decided where I was going to go to college. Weeks before graduating, I gave him a call, and right after my graduation, we began to talk on the phone a lot. The chemistry was amazing as we always had something to talk about. We really enjoyed each other's phone conversation. I was always a fun-loving and outgoing young lady. I loved to dress up and always got compliments on how I dressed. He was one of the ones always giving me compliments of how I looked. He always made me feel good about myself and continuously complimented me on my smile. Now that we were getting closer and talking a lot, I needed to know what his plans were for his future. We weren't in that same environment anymore, so I wasn't sure if he was still a street distributer or what. Now that I was older and wiser, I knew what that profession was and how bad it was to be in. I understood the dangers and trouble that came with it. I knew that I didn't want to deal with anyone in that profession, and I told him as much. He assured me that he had left that life and was actually looking for a trade to get into. I had one prior relationship before him that didn't last long. As you can imagine, with so many restrictions and at such a young age, it wasn't much of a real relationship. This one actually felt like it was going to be a start of a beautiful something.

My plans were to go to a local college but stay on campus. It was going to be such a big step for me and the most freedom that I was going to have in my entire life. Despite the fact that my parents became more lenient in high school, they still had a very tight grip on us. I was so happy that despite all their objections, I wasn't letting up. My first couple of months in college went pretty well. I wasn't the partying type and really wanted to focus on school. The kids at college were very wild, and it appeared that they were feeling just as caged as I was. It was definitely lots of drinking and partying in which I had no desire to be a part of at that time. I was able to still maintain one of my jobs I had while I was in high school. Mr. Mysterious and I were talking and spending lots of time together but just getting to know each other on the phone. I knew eventually I would spend time with him but didn't want to rush into it. We didn't have a title, so I considered him my very close friend. I was really enjoying making new friends, having my freedom, and getting to know him as much as possible. He wasn't very insisting and just seemed to go with the flow. He always asked me to spend the night with him, but I wasn't ready for that and didn't want to lose my focus on school. I had early morning classes and was doing very well in school. I also imagined that he would want to have sex, and I didn't feel I was ready to do that with him. I was making so many bad choices with whom I was letting get close to me it felt like I needed to give him slow access.

More time had passed, and the feelings were just getting stronger and stronger. I would say we were getting closer to about eleven months in, and he asked me to come out and have dinner with him. It was a Friday night and no school the next day. This would have been our actual first date as time didn't really permit for us to spend time together. I was anxious and really looking forward to having dinner with him. I was usually expected to come home for the weekends, but this time I just told my parents I had lots of studying that required my undivided attention. Of course, with lots of resistance from them, I was finally able to get them to see it my way. Finally, with them out of the way, I could give my undivided attention to him and dinner. Thank goodness I didn't have a curfew or have to cut our time together short. He came to pick me up from my campus, and we went to get something to eat. Dinner was lots of fun, but the time seemed to pass by so fast. He suggested that we go back to his house and just hang out. I was pretty against the idea, especially the fact that my parents would be right around the corner. Despite the fact they had no idea where he lived at, I just had that paranoia that we would somehow run into them. He convinced me how silly that was, and I decided to go to his house. We got to his house, and I was amazed at how beautiful the house was. I had never been in the previous house he lived before, but this one was like a mansion. It was almost like he was rich; I definitely didn't expect for him to live here. We got in pretty late, so it appeared everyone had been sleeping.

I was very nervous and really hoped that he didn't have any expectations. He appeared to be really into me and, so far, respected the limitations I had in place. We went to his room, and I have to say it was pretty impressive. He made me comfortable and said we could leave whenever I was ready. He sat on the recliner next to his bed as I lay on his bed watching TV. He had a couple of drinks and asked me if I wanted some. I had a few drinks before despite the fact I wasn't the drinking age. I was introduced to it by my older cousin who wanted my sister and me to do it with her as we were always curious. She always advised us not to do it at all, but since we were so curious, me especially, she wanted us to do it under her supervision. It was enjoyable for me, but my sister hated it. So needless to say, when he offered, I accepted. My drink of choice was Amaretto Sour, but unfortunately, he didn't know how to make that. All he had were pretty strong drinks, in which I'd never had before. I had a couple but didn't want to drink too much as I wasn't much of a drinker. He drank the rest of the night, and I only had about two. He offered more, but I declined, and he never tried to pressure me or convince me to want more. Seeing as he had too much, he wouldn't be able to drive me home. He offered to call me a taxi to get me back to school, but I declined. I felt so comfortable with him I wanted to spend the night. He was pretty wasted, exhausted, and didn't appear to have any much energy left. He got me a T-shirt and asked me if I wanted him to sleep on the recliner. I told him I trusted him and didn't mind sharing the bed with him. He held me the whole night, and we slept the night away. I slept so peacefully as he didn't try a thing. He put some music on and couldn't believe his taste in music. He played Maxwell's "This Woman's Work."

The night went perfect, and I woke up to him kissing me on my forehead. As we stared into each other's eyes, he told me how happy he was that I was here. I was happy to be in his arms. I was looking forward to spending more time with him and couldn't wait to be with him again. We had a couple more weekends like this together, and I felt I wanted to be with him every weekend. Finally, one weekend together and our passion together was uncontrollable. We kissed the night away, and it became really heated. He asked me if I was ready, and I felt like it was the right time. He waited so patiently and never pressured me to do anything I didn't want to do. He was always so kind and always made sure I was OK. The timing just felt right, and I knew that I wanted to be with him. I opened myself, and we made passionate love. It was really passionate and magical. That magical moment we spent together, I knew I never wanted it to end. He asked me to be his girlfriend the following morning, and I accepted. Whenever I wasn't at school or work, I wanted to spend time with him. We really enjoyed each other's company and became almost inseparable. I was falling in love with him and loved every moment of it. He was just my kind of guy, and I wanted every bit of him. He was always so nice, considerate, funny, and romantic. We're planning another weekend together, but I told him I needed to study because I had a test coming up. He promised to help me study in which I looked forward to seeing the studious side of him. I got to his house early that Friday in hopes of getting as much studying done. I had to work that weekend and wanted as much study time as possible. I got to his house, and it was nothing but playtime for him. He couldn't keep his hands off me and definitely didn't help me study. I urged him to help me focus because if not, I would have to leave.

I shouldn't have expected anything different from him. How could I forget the young man who never took school or adults seriously? I called a taxi while he was in the shower and left as he was getting out. He really didn't take me studying or wanting to leave seriously. Well, he learned pretty quickly that I wasn't playing around. I gave him a kiss on the lips with the towel wrapped around his waist and told him I would call him later. I got so caught up in my studies that I fell asleep on my books. I even woke up later than usual to get ready for work and barely making it on time. Thankfully I was able to get my studying done and made it to work on time. It was the middle of the day, and I was getting ready to go to lunch. I worked at a clothing store where there was a lot of men coming in and out. My job was to help and assist them in any way I could. I have to admit there was a lot of cute ones who flirted and came in frequently. It was flattering, and just barely starting this relationship, I didn't really know his likes and dislikes. Well, I was about to find out now.

I was a little late for lunch because I was helping a customer and a pretty cute one, I might add. Just as we were in mid flirting, I saw the customer looking over my shoulder. I turned around, and there was Mr. Mysterious, my now boyfriend, just angrily staring at us. The customer I was helping said, "My man, you okay. She's helping me." He completely ignored the guy and turned his attention and stares toward me. It was so awkward the customer asked me if I knew this weird motherfucker. As soon as those words came out of the customer's mouth, my boyfriend angrily asked him, "What the fuck did you just say?" I was so surprised by his anger as I'd never seen it before. I apologized to the customer and told him I had to leave. Not saying a word to him, I just stormed away from the both of them. I was already late for lunch, and that was where I was headed. He was following behind me and loudly asking me who that guy was. I begged him to please keep it down and not make a scene at my job. As soon as we got outside, he forcefully grabbed my arms and told me to slow down. The tone and anger in which he was talking to me was so unexpected. I urged him to calm down and let him know that I didn't like the way he was talking to me. I was pretty upset and began to rapidly feel uncomfortable with his behavior. He immediately saw how my mood was starting to change and began adjusting his attitude. I asked him what he was doing at my job to begin with because

I didn't know he was coming. He told me he came to apologize for disturbing my studying and felt horrible with how I left. He knew when my lunch break was and came to surprise me to take me to lunch. He apologized for his behavior and told me how much it bothered him to see me talking to another man. He said the guy was clearly into me, and it didn't help that I was dressed all sexy. I immediately told him not to go there as he never had a problem with how I dressed before. He asked me to come by his house later to explain himself as we spent all my break going back and forth. I told him that I had a lot of studying to do, and I could probably come by the following weekend.

A couple of days went by, and I was expecting him to fall back a little until I meet up with him on the up and coming weekend. Apparently, he couldn't wait until the following weekend and began just randomly showing up to my job. He was no longer coming inside; he would just wait for me outside during my lunch break. It was kind of creepy because he would just show up without even telling me. We had just started getting to know each other, and seeing that jealous side of him really turned me off. I believe he felt me pulling away, and him seeing me every day until I came to his house was his reassurance I wouldn't deviate from the plan. I almost wanted to cancel the weekend, but seeing how hard he was trying to make things right kept me from doing that. After all, we did just start dating and still getting to know each other. I rationalized for him and told myself there was really no need to cut him off like that. I really did like him a lot and enjoyed spending time with him. This was something that I told myself was just his way of expressing his feelings and kind of cute.

The weekend was here, and I was a little excited to spend time with him. I almost forgot why I was mad at him in the first place. He picked me up Friday evening from campus, and we headed straight to his house. We stopped and got some food and liquor. So far, the night was going pretty well, just as I hoped it would go. He was doing a little more drinking than usual, but it seemed all in fun. I wanted to bring up how he acted at my job but kind of felt like it was a one-time occurrence. We ate, watched movies, and surprisingly, he brought up the incident at my job himself. He started with an apology in which I accepted.

Shockingly, he asked me if I didn't think I owed him an apology also. I really thought he was joking and busted out in laughter. I got up to go to the bathroom, literally about to pee on myself because I thought it was really funny. As I was walking to the bathroom, he appeared to be getting really angry as he asked me, "What's so funny?" He was now insisting that I give him an apology and started making suggestions that I was fucking the customer I was helping. I was in total shock that he would suggest something so disrespectful. I now became defensive, and we were just shouting back and forth. I proceeded to walk away and gather my things. As I looked at him to say goodbye, I just saw his fist going right to my face. The powerful punch landed in my eyes, sending me to the ground. Balling up into a fetal position, also in such a state of shock, I was on the ground holding my eyes and crying. The pain was so hard it felt like my eyes had come out of the socket.

He immediately fell to the ground and attempted to hold me. I screamed, "Get the fuck off me! You are a fucking monster! Why would you do that to me?" He was pretty upset and continued to try and grab me. He was begging me to keep quiet as he lived with his grandmother and younger siblings. He said if she heard us, she wouldn't allow me to come here anymore but never said she would call the cops on him. Like I mentioned before, the house was like a mansion, so he had his own private area, where we didn't run into his family much of the times that I was there. However, the walls weren't soundproof, and they could hear any extremely loud noise we would make. "I'm so sorry. I didn't mean to. I have no idea what came over me," he cried to me. "I want to go home! Take me back! I don't want to be here!" I screamed. I was in a state of shock and just wanted to stay on the floor and process what just happened.

I don't understand why he just punched me in the face. I asked him to leave me alone as I lay on the floor back in the fetal position. I felt his hands on my back, and he was not leaving my side. At this point, I was too exhausted to tell him to stop touching me. I just wanted the pain to go away. He ran downstairs to get me an ice pack (well, some ice in a bag), and my first instinct was to just gather my things, call a cab, and leave. I couldn't move. I was paralyzed by the pain and the shock combined. He apologized the entire night and began crying almost as much as I was. He continued to explain. "I'm just so scared to lose you. I wasn't thinking straight. I was drinking so much that my emotions took over. Please don't leave me." He was begging at this point, followed by at least saying sorry one hundred times or more. The crazy thing is, I never thought to call the cops. I just wanted to leave and never see him again. He cried so much I started feeling sorry for him. It began to feel like I was the one who hit him. I lay on the floor for the entire night and had no idea how I was going to get through the day tomorrow because I had to go to work. Too mentally and physically exhausted to leave, I just wanted to sleep the night away.

D. SAULS

CHAPTER 5

THE LIES

I WOKE UP IN the morning in excruciating pain. I could barely open my eyes. As I was still lying on the floor, I woke up to him lying right next to me. He looked at me and said, "Oh shit, I'm so sorry, babe!" I became very anxious and scared to see what my face looked like. I finally got up to go to the bathroom and take a shower. I thought maybe if I had a nice hot bath, I would feel better enough to at least go to work. When I got to the bathroom and looked in the mirror, I began screaming. My eye was bloodshot red and black and blue. I definitely couldn't go to work like this. I wasn't sure how long it was going to take for it to go away, but I needed some time. It was so painful I wanted to go to the hospital, but, of course, he convinced me every reason why I shouldn't. He told me they wouldn't understand that he was drunk, and it was a mistake. He told me to just take some time off, and he would nurse my eye back to health. I had to go to school but did take four days off from work. He showed me how to cover up my eye, suggesting I wore sunglasses, and that way, no one would notice. If anyone did ask, he said to just tell them I walked into a door or I got hit with a ball in the face. I told him those were pretty silly lies, and who would believe that stupidity? He assured me that they were pretty believable, and no one would really question them. I asked him how did he know so well what lies would cover up a black eye? Had he done this before? He assured me that he had never hit another woman, and I was the first. He said he was so deeply in love with me and was never scared to lose anyone before. He promised me that this would never happen again, and if it wasn't for the mere fact that he was drunk, it wouldn't have happened in the first place. He seemed so sincere, and after all, as I stated, he was drinking more than usual. It all made sense and too easy to believe that he would never do it again.

It had been four days now, and I had to call out from work as the bruise was too fresh. I couldn't wear sunglasses to work, but I was able to wear them at school, already strategizing that I would sit in the back toward the corner and socialize less. So the incident happened on Friday, and I didn't have to go back to school until Monday. I called out from work Saturday to Tuesday and went to school with shades on Monday. As the days went by, the black eye started to fade away but still noticeable. I finally had to go back to work on Wednesday because I really couldn't afford to call out for too many days. It was also but so many days I could miss without my sister getting really worried and wanting to physically see me. I needed the money for my bare necessities, didn't want to take advantage of the understanding of my boss, and didn't want my sister worrying. I had pretty good work ethics, which was noticeable to everyone that mattered. I'd been there for years and until this incident had never called out from work, let alone calling out for so many days at a time.

I didn't discuss much of my business with my dorm mates and kind of kept a low profile. My dorm mates were pretty cool, but I didn't feel like I could really share with them what was going on with me. I had one whom I was getting pretty close with, but I was still hesitant to share my story. I came back to the school very upset and jittery. She asked if I was OK and told me that if I wanted to talk about anything, she was there for me. I really appreciated her offer but was surprised that she even offered that. I thought I was doing a good job in hiding everything. She was never pushy, but I noticed that she started giving me more attention than usual. I started feeling like maybe one day I could tell her what was going on with me but not yet. I kept my conversations to a quick hello and always appeared to be in a rush. That way, they wouldn't have time to question me or ask me why I was always wearing those shades. I have to say I did a pretty good job in hiding it. I was hoping the bruising would go away soon so I could stop wearing these stupid shades. Got me out here looking like an FBI agent concealing her identity.

Wednesday morning was here, and I walked into work with my shades on, in fear of removing them. Unfortunately, I knew that I was going to have to remove them soon. It didn't help that when I checked the schedule, they had me at the register. Oh no, my black eye couldn't be an open display for everyone who came in the store to see. I had to be hidden where too much attention wouldn't be drawn to me. I immediately asked the floor manager if I could just be on the floor. She didn't hesitate to accommodate me but did immediately notice my eye. We were in the back office, away from our coworkers. She grabbed my face and asked me, "What happened to your eye, honey?" I immediately told her that I was playing ball and got hit in the face with a ball. She smirked and said, "No, sweetie, that's not what happened. Did that asshole you've been hanging with lately do this to you? I've seen a change in you as soon as you started dealing with him. You're a beautiful young lady known for your fashion sense. You don't even dress how you used to. He's bringing you down. I'm ten years older than you, and I've heard this story already. A ball wouldn't cause you that kind of bruising. Leave before it's too late! I promise you, sweet young lady, it's doesn't get better." I was looking at her and in disbelief that she was able to see right through me. I wanted so bad to tell her what happened to me and that everything she said was right, but something in me wanted to protect him more than anything.

You didn't see how much he cried and how hurt he felt. It wasn't his fault; it was the excessive drinking that made him do this to me. We were dating for a while, and I'd never seen anything but kindness and understanding from him. How could I not give him another chance? That day, every single person I encountered asked me about my eye, in which I told them the same sorry. I told the lie so much it started to feel like the truth to me. My sister, however, I couldn't lie to. I mean, I tried, but she was like my manager and saw right through me. After my attempts to lie to her failed, I immediately told her what happened. I did my best to make her believe that it wasn't his fault, and he promised to never do it again. My sister said that he shouldn't have done it to begin with, and she didn't care that he was drinking. It didn't matter what anyone said to me; I had already agreed that I was going to forgive him.

I believed him when he told me he would never do it again. I really believed that it was the alcohol that made him do it. She insisted on me never seeing him again, and unfortunately, I couldn't guarantee that me not seeing him anymore was going to happen. I was already deeply emotionally invested in him.

A couple of months went by, and he had been on his best behavior. I can't begin to tell you how extremely nice he was to me. He was catering to my every need, and it felt good. It definitely was a distraction from that black eye he gave me. It began to be a memory in the past for me, almost like it never happened. I was really enjoying this new him that was trying so hard to make up for what he did. It was beginning to feel like the first time we started dating all over again. My heart was beating for him all over again, and I looked forward to spending the weekends I had free with him. I really enjoyed my younger brother and didn't really get to spend as much time with him like I would have wanted to. I was always so focused on being free, I didn't realize that meant leaving him behind. Some weekends, I would go home and spend time with him, and the weekends that I wasn't with my brother, I would spend with my boyfriend. It got to the point where I didn't want to miss time spent with my brother or my boyfriend. I figured the best way to handle that dilemma was to bring my brother along at times we were spending together. He didn't seem to mind and actually enjoyed spending time with my brother. It was a win-win for me as things started to look up for our relationship. He really was sorry and did everything in his power to show me that he loved me enough to change.

By now, my eye was fully healed, and there weren't as many questions as before. The one person other than my sister who stuck on the inquiries was my manager at work. She was a really nice and caring lady, but it was becoming a little too overwhelming, especially after the fact that months went by, and he had been on his best behavior. She asked me if I finally decided to leave him because she didn't see him around anymore. Of course, she did not know that I gave him a heads-up that people at work were already suspecting that he was the one who gave me the black eye. With that information alone, he decided that he didn't want the negative attention and did stop coming to my job. I told her that we were still together and assured her that he had changed. Since that one time he hit me, it hadn't happened since then. He was drinking a lot when he hit me, I reminded her. She assured me that it would happen again. He was just waiting to get me back to being comfortable. "They don't change. They never do," she assured me. I was curious to know why it was so hard for her to believe that he could change. It felt like she knew him personally and was speaking her truth from that. I had to ask her why she was so negative toward him. She told me that she knew from experience as she watched someone very close to her go through the exact same thing. She could tell I was a little annoyed with her persistence as she told me that she would stop bothering me. "What you do with your life is your business," she told me. "I only talk to you because I've grown fond of you and really care about you. You're an amazing, beautiful, and kind young lady. You can be with any man that would never even think of putting their hands on you. For your sake, I hope he does change, and I will leave it at that."

It didn't feel like he was going to do anything to hurt me. We were getting closer than we had ever been. I started revisiting with him what his career choice was going to be. He told me he was still working on it and that he would definitely want my help in figuring that out. I was excited to help him in his endeavors. We were still spending most weekends together, but I started forming study groups in which our time together would be less. He appeared to be supportive and said that my studies were just as important to him as they were to me. My studies became so overwhelming that some weekends we planned together, I had to cancel. One weekend in particular, he really urged me to change my mind as he expressed that he really wanted to see me and spend time with me. I told him that I would try to make it next weekend. I felt really bad that I had canceled and began seeing if I could move some things around to make the visit. Now I was filled with excitement that I was actually going to surprise him. I was looking forward to what his reaction was going to be when I showed up unexpectedly. I wondered if he would be just as excited to see me as I would be to see him. Well, only time would tell.

CHAPTER 6

DECEPTION

CELL PHONES BACK then weren't as popular as they are now. We had beepers, but you really couldn't communicate too much with a beeper. I wanted to give him a heads-up that I was coming, but I kind of wanted to surprise him more. I wasn't sure if he was going to be home or not, but that was a chance I was willing to take. If he wasn't home, once I got in, I would just rest and study until he got home, I told myself. Well, I got to his house, and his grandmother let me in because he wasn't home. We had a pretty good relationship, and she always referred to me as the nice young lady. When I arrived, it was early evening, about five or six in the evening. She stated the obvious that he wasn't home, but I could wait until he got home. "I don't know what time that will be, but you can stay as long as you want," she told me. Well, hours went by, which seemed pretty fast as I was well into my studies. I was starting to realize that he might not be coming home at all. A couple more hours passed, and he was still not home. I was really tired and kind of upset that he hadn't returned home yet. I was at the point of wondering where the hell he could be and what was keeping him so late. I really wanted to surprise him and spend time with him. The later it became, that would mean the less time I would have to spend with him. Now despite the fact I said I would stay until he got home, even if it meant spending the night, I was starting to rethink that decision.

Just as I made the final decision to actually leave, I heard voices and more than his footsteps. Unfortunately, I heard voices of like four or five other guys accompanying him. It was already about 10:00 or 11:00 p.m., and I was wondering why the hell they would be coming home with him so late. I definitely didn't want to surprise him with a whole bunch of other guys, so I quickly ran into his large walk-in closet. I knew that he would have no idea I was hiding in there if I stayed extra quiet. Thank goodness it was big enough where I could stretch out. Plus I had my books with me, so I could still continue my studies until they left. However, now I was thinking that would be pretty creepy if I came out of the closet after they left. He would probably think that I had completely lost my mind. One hour went by, and it was just a bunch of loud talking, drinking, and playing games. I was starting to get pretty tired and afraid that if I fell asleep, I would probably start snoring, and all of them would know I was hiding in the closet. Just as I started to dose off, I was awakened by their loud laughter. Oh my goodness, I couldn't believe they were all still here and started wondering if they were going to have a fucking sleepover. Just as I was wondering and contemplating if at this point I should just walk out as I was getting really tired of being in the closet, it sounded like they were all making their way out the door and leaving, and he was walking them outside.

I breathed a sigh of relief as I anxiously exited the closet. It was pretty late, almost one in the morning. I couldn't believe I waited so long to actually see him, but it would make it that much more exciting once he came back to the room and saw me laid out in nothing but my underwear, waiting on his bed. At least I hoped that would be the case. As soon as I exited the closet, my heart just sank right into my stomach. I was squinting and rubbing my eyes as to ensure what I was seeing was real. "Is that a white powdery substance in a bag?" I was asking myself. As I came closer and closer to the table where the white powdery substance lay, all my doubts of what it could be was confirmed. At this point, I was pissed and just started gathering my things to leave before he knew that I was even there. I finally gathered all my belongings and on my way out the door. I opened the door to exit, and at that exact same time, he was entering. We stared into each other's eyes, but mine were full of tears. He was so excited, happy to see me, and asked me when I arrived. I was speechless and offered him no response. He appeared puzzled as he asked me why I was crying. I asked him to please get out of my way. He continued asking what was wrong with me. I was telling him that it would be best if he would just let me leave because I didn't want to talk about it. He insisted on me not leaving and pushed me back into the room. As soon as he brought me back into the room, he caught on immediately why I was upset. I guess at that moment, it didn't sink in what he left just lying on his table.

He said, "I can explain, just please let me explain. It's not what you think." I looked at him with such disappointment and asked him just how stupid he thought I was. At this point, I didn't want to hear anything he had to say. I would have to be really blind and stupid to misconstrue what I knew I saw. I screamed, "What could you possibly have to tell me that can explain what appears to be a bag of fucking cocaine or crack on your table! I'm sorry I can't tell the difference!" I proceeded to ask him, "All this time you told me you were going to take up a trade and that you left that drug life behind was a fucking lie?" How more deceiving can you get than this? Here it is I believed that he was really looking to change his life around. I expressed how I didn't want to deal with anyone in that type of lifestyle, and he assured me he wasn't. I really didn't ask too many questions; I would just take everything he told me at face value. What a lying piece of shit this guy is! He proceeded to tell me that it was not his and that he was holding it for his friends. "So why couldn't they hide it at their place? Why were you the only option?" I asked. He told me that his house was the better option because it was in more of a suburbia area and lesser chance for anyone to suspect it was here. Oh OK, so I guess this supposed to make it make sense to me. It was OK for you to hold it for them as long as you were not selling. "Oh OK, now that makes it OK," I say sarcastically. "I'm done and not entertaining anything you have to say right now. Please let me go. I really don't want to be here, especially in a room full of drugs."

He insisted on not letting me go and assured me it was going to be gone in a couple of hours. I was urging him to just let me walk away and that it would be best for the both of us. The more he tried to refrain me from leaving, the more anxious I became. I'd never been around nor had I ever seen drugs up close and personal. It was nerve-racking to be in the room with it and in such proximity. Really bad thoughts were running through my mind as I fought against it. The consequences if I executed the actions in my thoughts wouldn't be good. I needed to get out of there, or I was going to explode. Why did I come here in the first place? I should have just stayed on campus. I'd never surprised him before and didn't even know if he would have been pissed or happy. He had come unannounced to my job so many times, so I didn't really think it would have been a big deal. I should have thought this through a little more before I made the decision to surprise him based solely on my emotions.

Powder was flying everywhere just as his hands flew right across my face. My face tingled as I felt the vibration of the loud smack. Everything appeared to be in slow motion as he was screaming, "What the fuck did you just do! Why did you do that!" "I told you to let me go! I told you I didn't want to be fucking here! You were holding me against my will! What did you think was going to happen!" He pulled me by my hair with his hands on my throat and threw me on the bed. "I told you this wasn't mine! Do you have any idea what the fuck this shit cost?" I knew that with so much outrage, I wasn't thinking rationally. I played it over and over in my head what the outcome would be if I emptied the whole bag on the floor, flushed it down the toilet, or threw it out the window. That was why I warned him and told him to leave me alone and let me go. He was pacing back and forth at this time, and I was terrified that there was more to come than just the smack and pulling of the hair. He began to salvage as much as he could but not having to salvage much. All I did was smack the bag off the table, and it just so happened to have a big whole in it. How was I supposed to know that it was going to go flying in the air? I got up to leave, and he attempted to stop me again by pushing me back on the bed. At this point, I was screaming, and it was probably about three in the morning. His grandmother heard the yelling and came knocking on the door. He yelled through the door that we were okay and just messing around. I immediately responded and said, "I'm so sorry. I'm coming out right now and about to leave." I ran to quickly open the door as I knew he wouldn't try anything with his grandmother right at the door.

What had I gotten myself into? He promised that he would never hit me again. I was thankful that it was my cheeks and not my eyes this time. It took so long for that black eye to go away. I dreaded having to make up another lie as I didn't know what a good lie would be for a bruise on your cheek. Well, maybe he wouldn't have hit me this time if I didn't try to destroy his drugs (well, as he put it, his friends). I was replaying the whole moment in my head and actually justifying him slapping me. I found myself to be pretty lucky that he didn't do worse. I was starting to feel bad and blaming myself for his actions. It wouldn't have never happened if I didn't just show up to his place unannounced. I also knew that I would have never found out that he was lying to me the entire time he told me he left that life behind him. Whatever the case might be, I was actually hoping that he wasn't mad at me. When I arrived on campus from that morning from his house, I immediately went to the bathroom and looked in the mirror. I remember thinking that it wasn't that bad as my face was just red and the skin a little swollen. I didn't expect the swelling to last too long or be noticeable at all. I wanted to call him and had the crazy urge to talk to him. I knew I wasn't going to be the one to call him but didn't plan on refusing his calls. Now that I had calmed down, I actually wanted to talk to him and hear what he had to say. I didn't want to believe he was deceiving me about getting his life back on track the honest way. He seemed so sincere and convincing I wanted everything he told me to be true. I didn't want to believe that he was the master of deceptions.

I waited for him to call me, but weeks went by and no call. I was starting to feel like it was for the best. I really messed up for him not to call me or even try to ask for an apology. At least that was what I was thinking in my head. He must've really thought that what I did was worth him not speaking to me. Now it was going on a full month since the incident happened and still no call from him. I was feeling kind of confused because I knew that despite the powder appearing to fly everywhere, the bag was still pretty full. Under the circumstances, after that vibrating slap he gave me, he should at least have felt sorry for that. Come to think of it, he never apologized and was way more concerned with the fate of the drugs than me. Oh well, I guess I would just leave well enough alone.

D. SAULS

CHAPTER 7

PROMISES

I WAS FIVE HOURS into my studying, getting ready for exams I had in a couple of days. I found myself drifting away in my thoughts. I was feeling kind of sad that it was going on one month now, and I hadn't heard from him, but I knew with time, the sadness shall pass. I would just focus on me and my studies and leave the past in the past. It was kind of mind-boggling that I would even still be thinking about him like this. We hear the saying "Why do good girls like bad boys?" all the time. I never thought that this would be my continuous story of choosing the bad ones. I would do better and give the good ones an actual chance. I had met so many studious and handsome ones asking me out, so many regulars who would come to my job just to see me. It was a bonus for the clothing store I worked at the time because in trying to impress me, they would always purchase something. I promised myself that I would do better with the men who occupied my space. I promised myself that I would do better with the men whom I share my thoughts with. I promised myself that I wouldn't share my body with anyone else who wasn't worthy! I should have promised myself that I would never share myself with anyone else but my husband.

The promises to myself were going so well until they weren't. I was in full self-love mode, at least I thought I was. I was in my dorm room, just relaxing, chilling with my dorm mates. I got a buzz from the security desk, letting me know I had a visitor. I was kind of puzzled because I wasn't expecting anyone, but sometimes my sister would randomly stop by. I went downstairs to sign whoever this visitor was in. In the dorms, you have to actually come down to sign your guess in. I don't know why I didn't just ask the guard who it was. I guess I was so anxious to know who it was I leaped before walking. As soon as I got off the elevator and see who was standing there, my heart dropped to my stomach. Yes, it appears I was having so many moments that were dropping my heart to my stomach. I'm surprised it didn't get stuck there. I wanted to just close the elevator shut and go back upstairs before he even saw me. Unfortunately, it was too late as soon as the elevator door opened, our eyes met. He had the stupidest smile on his face while I was barely smiling. I was surprised to see him but wasn't happy. In the beginning, I felt like I was missing him, but some time had pass, and that was enough for me to miss him less.

Other than picking me up and dropping me off, this was the first time he had ever actually step foot in the building. I asked him what he was doing here. He could tell I was a little off and not too happy to see him. At this point, I already felt it was too late. I already made these promises to myself, and they didn't include him. It was almost like he felt himself fading in my memories and needed to insert himself back in. I opened the door and stepped outside and asked him to follow me. There was no way I was letting him into my dorm room. I didn't feel comfortable with giving him that kind of access, and I didn't trust him enough. He asked me why we were standing outside and not going upstairs. I let him know that he couldn't just come to my dorm room like that. I told him that I didn't know if he was holding any packages for any friends, and that shit wasn't following me to my dorm room. He was very upset when I made that comment and began to charge toward me. I immediately started walking back in the eyesight of the guard in case he got any crazy ideas. "You really shouldn't be here, and I would really appreciate if you leave and don't come back," I told him. He was getting angrier, but I couldn't tell if it was because of what I was saying or that he couldn't really hit me with the guard booth right in front of us. I started to walk away from him, telling him to have a good night. He yanked my arm so hard, bringing me toward him and away from the guard's view.

I was flinching because I expected some sort of slap or punch to follow. I was pretty scared at this point and began to raise my voice really loud, telling him to get the fuck away from me. He placed his hands on my mouth and begged me not to scream. He said, "Just listen, please. I need you to just listen. I know I was wrong and that I disappointed you. I didn't come here to fight nor hurt you. I was doing good until you almost disappeared that product into the air. It wasn't mine like I told you, and it could have cost me some serious trouble with whom I was holding it for. I really didn't mean to hit you, and I'm really trying to get my life back on the right track. I never had somebody that believes in me like you do, and I can't do it without you." He was saying all the right words, and I wanted to believe him but still having my doubts. He grabbed me and began kissing me as he promised that he would try and be whatever man I needed him to be, begging for one more chance. At this point, he became teary-eyed and softened my stance against him. "Give me some time to think about this," I told him. "I'm really not ready to make a decision right now. I'll call you later." And as I proceeded to walk away, he said, "So you really not going to let me come upstairs with you? What, you got a man up there or something?" I just looked at him, shook my head, and told him that was exactly why I had to think about it. I urged him to go home and assured him that I would call him soon. "I really don't want you to make a scene in front of my school, and the people here are really nosy," I told him. Thank God he didn't push the issue and gave me a kiss and left.

As we were outside, my dorm mate whom I told you guys I was getting closer to walked by and saw us outside. She walked over and said hello and didn't even acknowledge him or stop long enough for me to introduce him. Once I got back upstairs, my brain was on overload. I had no idea at this point what to do. I wanted to get rid of him and just move on. I was actually headed in that direction until he so easily just showed up and derailed my entire plan. My dorm mate came to my room as I was sitting on my bed, just staring into space. Fortunately for me, I had a roommate who was hardly there. She plopped right on my bed and said, "I'm not trying to be in your business, but who was that dusty ass guy you were talking to? Please tell me that's not your boyfriend. All these guys who been trying to talk to you, please tell me he's not the reason none of them could get no play!" At this point, I was laughing so hard because I honestly didn't expect her to come at me like that. She was so blunt and didn't care what words were coming out her mouth about him. She freely told me, "I don't like him for you, and I know he's the reason why you were wearing those shades for so long, when you've never worn them before." I looked at her with such shock and just began crying. How could she possibly know without me having to say a word. I just fell into her lap and just cried uncontrollably. She just held me, wiped my tears, and told me that I was too beautiful of a soul to ever go through something like this.

It felt so good to finally let it out without having to say much. She then began to confide in me and share with me the tragedies in her life. She surprisingly revealed, "Having dealt with a drug-addicted mother, being homeless, watching abuse after abuse, and close to death, it's easy for me to detect these things." I couldn't believe she was sharing such private moments of her life with me. If you looked at her, you would never know that she'd been through any of those things. She always carried herself so well, her fashion sense was on point, her hair always looked amazing, and her sense of humor was always there. I remember thinking how someone who'd been through all that be so happy all the time. I knew her willingness to share was to get me to open up. Well, I have to say it worked. I began to share with her from the beginning of him being my crush to that first unexpected punch. We both began to cry as so much heartache was shared. It felt like so much weight was lifted off my shoulder as she was the first and only person I could share every detail with at the time. I couldn't share it with my sister because I knew it would be too painful for her to see me going through anything like this. I was just happy that I could talk to someone and not feel judged. As I explained the story out loud and hearing myself talk, I almost felt ashamed of the person I was who was allowing for such things to happen to me.

"Promise me that you won't deal with him anymore," she said. I told her I couldn't make that promise because I really loved him. "I can't make that promise to you especially when I can't even make it to myself." She told to just be careful because he was not going to change. She said, "You're too nice and pretty to be dealing with such a loser, but I can't make you see it. Hopefully you will see it for yourself sooner than later." I felt the same way, but this guy had a hold on me that I just couldn't shake. He didn't have to do much to get me running right back to him. Even though I didn't let him see how weak he had me, he did. A couple of days went by since his unexpected visit, and I didn't call him like I said I would. After having that conversation with my dorm mate, I began thinking if talking to him was the right thing to do. He was already out of my life. Why would I let him back in? Every reason not to deal with him was right in front of me, so why was my heart telling me otherwise? I was back to feeling like how I felt before he showed up at my dorm. I knew that I was going to have to communicate that to him eventually. How he would take it would definitely be a different story. I could only hope that he would take it in peace, but every bone in my body told me that he wouldn't.

I was trying to build the courage up to go and talk to him. I knew what I wanted to say but didn't know how to say it. I knew that news like that couldn't be told while I was alone with him as I had no idea what he would do. It was Friday afternoon, and I'd decided that I would catch a taxi to his house. I just got out of class, and it was still pretty early where everyone at his house would still be up, so it should be safe to say what I needed to say. I didn't plan on showing up unexpected this time, so I called before making plans to go over there. Unfortunately, when I called, he wasn't home. I just took it as it wasn't meant for us to talk at all and the sign that I needed to walk away clean. Just as the thought crossed my mind, the buzzer went off in our dorm room, and it was for me. At this time, I just knew that it was him and started to feel really nervous. "I guess this is a good thing that he's here," I told myself. We did need to talk, and I just had to be really direct with him. I hated that he once again after being told not to show up at my dorm at all, let alone unannounced, despite that fact I knew that I wasn't going to make it into a big deal. I came downstairs with the intentions of getting away from my campus dorm so we could talk. As soon as I came off the elevator, I walked straight out the door, not even saying hello. He followed me outside and said, "You just gonna walk right past me and not even say anything?" "I saw you, and you saw me. I told you not to show up like this, but you do anyway. How do you expect me to act?" I said I wasn't going to make it a big deal, but he pissed me off questioning me about saying some damn hello.

I got into his car, and he reached over to kiss me. "I missed you so much," he said. "We need to talk," I told him. "Okay, well, let's talk right here in the car." I didn't feel comfortable talking in the car, so I suggested that we go to a park and talk. He didn't want to go to the park and suggested that we just go to his house and walk around the block. I was comfortable with doing that. Before we pulled off, he asked me where my overnight bag was. I told him I wasn't spending the night and that I just wanted to talk. He led with "I love you, and I want to change, but it feels like you already gave up on me. I understand if you did, but you didn't give me a chance to prove myself." I was listening with open ears and asked him, "How many chances do you need to prove yourself? I already told you I'm not dating no drug dealer, and you assured me you left that life. Yet I found you with drugs in your house! You promised that you would never hit me again, and yet you've already done it twice." He cut me off and said, "The second one didn't count. You caught me off guard, and that was my reflexes reacting." I was shocked that he would even say that to me and not even show any remorse. Then he proceeded to reiterate. "I told you those drugs weren't mine and that I was holding them for my friend." I told him that didn't matter. I asked him, "If you got caught with the drugs by the cops, can you tell them you are holding it for a friend, and you can walk away free? No, so if that can't happen, what makes you think I would be OK with that stupid ass excuse?"

Walking ten feet ahead of him, I just came out and said it. "I don't want to be with you. It's just not going to work." He jokingly told me that I was his girl, and I was not going nowhere. I told him that I was not joking, and I really thought it was time that we move on. I started walking really fast back toward the house as I could see his mood was starting to change. Surprisingly, he said, "I can't make you stay, but before you leave me, can you spend just one more weekend with me?" The fact that he was so calm and taking it better than I expected, I didn't hesitate to say yes. I felt like that was the least I could do considering I was leaving him. I had some clothes left at his place, not a lot but enough that I didn't have to go back to the dorms to collect anything. We got to his room, and I saw all these different pamphlets for job trainings and trades. I have to admit I was pretty impressed. He saw the smile on my face and asked me if I could help him. "I'm going to change. You just have to give me a chance. Just one more chance, and I promise you I won't make you regret it." We began kissing, hugging, and the next thing I know, he was inside me. The sex was always good with him, and when we connected like that, it was like nothing else mattered. I knew after that happened I was going to give him another chance. I really wanted to believe that this time he was for real and everything he told me wasn't a lie. "Fuck it," I told myself. "I'll give him one more chance."

CHAPTER 8

BAD INFLUENCE

I NEVER UNDERSTOOD WHY he was living the way he was living. He appeared to have it so good. He lived in a house that was equivalent to a mansion. It was one of the most beautiful homes I ever did step foot in. He had a grandmother who loved him and siblings whom he got along well with. Why was he ever outside in the beginning selling drugs? His circumstances were different from the typical dealers out there trying to keep a roof over their heads or feed their children. He had a beautiful roof over his head and had no children to feed. He didn't share much with me about his past before. But it looked like he was really trying to help me understand him. Explaining to me that he had no father figure and his mother was a drug addict, he found himself getting love and attention from the streets. He didn't have the financial need; however, the streets were his home away from home. He expressed that those guys out there were the fathers he never had and the mothers who weren't on drugs. As he was out there on a daily basis, their mothers and fathers became his. At this point, I felt that he was misunderstood and helped me understand him a little better. Feeling sorry for all the pain he had been through, it made me sad for him and, in my mind, justified why even though he didn't mean it, it would occasionally hit me.

Feeling even more connected than before, I began spending more time with him than on campus. He drank and smoked a lot, and slowly but surely, I began to pick up his bad habits. It really holds true that you are the company you keep. I never in a million years thought that I would be smoking cigarettes, one of the most disgusting and unhealthy habits in my opinion anyone could have. It started off with me telling him to please stop or don't do it in front of me. It later turned to let me try one of those, followed by not being able to have a drink without one. I began to slowly start buying my own pack of cigarettes. We were eating takeout almost every time I was there, and I have to say it was nothing healthy. I still had to go to work and realized that none of my clothes were fitting. I was transforming into some fat cigarette smoking hood rat. I was almost unrecognizable at work and even to myself. I went from wearing the sexiest size 2s and 4s to now wearing baggy sweatpants. How fast did I transform from caring about the way I looked to not caring at all? OMG, I couldn't believe I was wearing sweatpants to work. I was no longer that hot sexy young lady whom everyone adored and always complimented. Instead, the guys would come to the store now and ask if I was pregnant or why did I let myself go like that. At this point, I didn't even care. All that mattered to me was that I was still sexy to him. It was so easy for him to strip of my pride and beauty without me even realizing it. I was always prideful in being respected and always took my time to maintain a nice presence. My self-esteem and love for myself was gone in a blink of an eye. He had me right where he wanted me. He was such a bad influence and looked like I was easily influenced.

Months went by since he told me that he was looking for a trade or something productive to do with his life. Remember those pamphlets he had lying around for me to help him with? Well, I did help him fill them out, but nothing ever got mailed out. It seemed as though those were put on display just for show. Yes, to show me that he was looking long enough to distract me for when he never fell short with the actual search. As soon as he saw how comfortable I was, he stopped talking about a trade. Every chance I got, I tried to encourage him, but he began to show how he really felt about that idea. He never took it seriously or had any intentions of following through. It became obvious that all that was just to shut me up and distract me. He knew how to play so many games, lie, and boy oh boy, was he the master of manipulation. He became like a drug to me, and I needed to be around him. I started losing sight of all things that were important. I began following a pattern of missing classes, drinking, and smoking. My grades started to slip, and my attendance at school was becoming less. What had become of me?

My father bought me a car for my sophomore year in college, and I carelessly would let him drive it. He got into a really bad accident with his car in which I later found out he was drinking and driving. He crashed his car and left the scene of the accident and reported it stolen. How stupid could I be to let this motherfucker drive the car that my dad bought me with his hard-earned money? To make matters even worse, I later found out that his license just recently got suspended. As soon as I found that out, I objected to him driving my car. Would you believe that he was insisting on still driving it despite the fact his license was suspended? Days went by after finding out about the suspension, and he asked me again if he could borrow the car. I kindly repeated no and told him that my answer wasn't going to change. "If you get caught driving my car without a license, who do you think will get in trouble?" Not to mention the car was under my father's name. I couldn't understand why he couldn't understand and respect when I said no. We ended the night with him saying that he now understood and wouldn't bother me again with asking to borrow my car. I told him that if I was free and he needed to go somewhere, I wouldn't mind taking him. I woke up the next morning, and he was not beside me. I immediately wake up looking for him, searching through the house, and he was nowhere to be found. His grandmother was up and asked me if I was OK. I told her I was OK but looking for her grandson. She told me he left since last night. "He's not back yet? I hope he's OK," she said. Now I was fuming and worried at the same time. I hoped he was OK but also hoped that nothing happened to the car. My dad would kill me if he found out something happened to the car. He consistently told me to be very careful with the car.

Hours went by, and I heard nothing from him. I had no way of contacting him and had no idea where he could be. I had to go to school soon but contemplating on if I would just skip school. I needed to know where he was at with my car. I was getting even more heated at the thought of me catching the bus or having to dish out money to pay for a taxi. I decided I wasn't going to do either and just wait for him to get home. It was now afternoon, and I was crying. I was crying so much but didn't know if he was OK or if something happened to the car. I knew there had to be pay phones wherever he was at. Why the hell hadn't he called me to at least let me know that he was OK? After all, he never even had my permission to take my car and knew that I had to be to school in the morning. It was clear to me that at this point, all he cared about was himself. So much time went by, and I was now at the point where I was thinking about calling the cops and reporting my car stolen. We were now almost into the evening time, and I was just picking up the phone to call the police. Just as I picked up the phone, I heard his voice. I ran out of the room and saw him sitting there in the kitchen talking to his grandmother as if he didn't just take my car without me knowing.

"Where's my car?" "Oh shit," he said. "You still here?" I was confused by his whole nonchalant attitude. I repeated again, "Where the fuck is my car?" I was so heated and couldn't even think straight. He gave me this smirk and pulled me away from the kitchen. He told me that he was so sorry that he took the car without my permission. He continued to tell me one of his boys got shot, and he needed to go to the hospital. Then oh yes, it got better. He went out drinking and got so drunk that someone stole the keys to my car. I couldn't believe the words that were coming out of his mouth. All I could think about was that the car was in my father's name and what kind of trouble he would be in. He sarcastically said, "Thanks for asking me if I'm OK, but don't worry about it. I reported the car stolen." My head at this point felt like it was about to burst, and I had no clue what to do at this point. I hated him and just wanted to punch him in the face but knew that I wasn't a match for him. I immediately walked away from him, called a taxi, and headed out the door. He followed me out the door and had the nerve to try and stop me from leaving. "Please leave me the fuck alone and get away from me."

I got to the dorms and in complete disarray. I was so heated that I began talking to my friend about the situation. I was so loud that everyone in our dorm apartment heard me. They all started gathering around to hear this crazy ass story. Collectively, they all suggested that

I report this to the police. I thought long and hard about it, and then I decided to take their advice. I never got the police involved before, but it looked like things were going to have to change. There was a blatant disregard for me and now my property. He didn't even care that it was in my father's name. I decided that the following morning, I was going to walk over to the campus police and file a complaint. As soon as the sun rose, right before class, I walked over to the campus police and explained to them what happened. I was completely disappointed when I was told that, first, it didn't happen here, so they couldn't take a complaint. Second, I was told that if he was my boyfriend and had the key, it would be hard to prove that he took it without my permission. Basically, it would be his word against mine. This couldn't be my life right now, I remember thinking. So clearly, now I was going to have to tell my father at some point. Of course, I would have to go with the obvious story that wasn't going to get me killed. I told my dad the car got stolen at school. He was disappointed but just asked if I was OK. The car was a pretty old car and only had liability. My dad said hopefully if they found it, it was not damaged. If it was, it wouldn't be covered, and I would just lose the car completely. It was so hard for me to hear that.

I was really disgusted with how he took my car while I was sleeping but even more upset that all he had to offer was sorry. "I don't want your fucking sorry!" I screamed. "You can pay me the money for my car, if they don't find it." At this point, I didn't even know if he was even telling the truth about the night my car went missing. It didn't make any sense to me that someone could just take the keys to your car and you don't even notice it. I felt in my heart he was lying but had no way of proving it. He agreed to replace the car if it wasn't found. I had a delayed reaction, and then I remembered he didn't have a job. I asked him how was he going to replace my car if he didn't even have a job. He assured me that he would get it from his grandmother and not to worry about it. At this point, I didn't care where he got it from as long as he replaced my car. That was all that mattered. Thankfully for me, I spoke to my dad a couple of days later, and the car was recovered with minor scratches. I had no faith in him that he would have replaced my car for me. I knew now from this point on that I would never leave my car keys lying around where he could find it. I also didn't plan on spending that much time with him after that incident. I was so done with him until I wasn't. I hated my indecisiveness with him. Just when I thought I would be free of him, I would let him pull me right back into his web of lies, abuse, and deception.

CHAPTER 9

THE FIRST AUDIENCE

I REALLY HAD NO desire to talk to him at this point. It was as if this was our new norm. He would do something that would upset me; I would stop talking to him for some time, months at a time. Eventually, he would come begging for my forgiveness, and I would take him back. It was expected for me to always take him back. He began to know me very well and all the right things to say to get me to come back. He would pull on my heartstrings as he knew that my heart was very big. He clearly took advantage of that, and I just let him. The semester for school had ended, and this year I decided not to take summer classes. After months of not talking to him, he came to tell me that he just enrolled in a medical billing course and wanted me to join it with him. This class wasn't going to take the whole summer. I was so proud of his initiative that I completely disregarded why I once again wasn't talking to him this time. I only wanted the best for him and knew that if he had his priorities in order, then maybe our relationship could be better than what it was. I had hope and wasn't giving up on us just yet. So much time had passed, and it was really starting to feel like somewhat of a normal relationship. The last time he hit me was so long ago. It appeared that he was holding true to his word.

The classes had started, and I was a little worried on how we were going to get there. It was a big distance away, and finances were really tight. I had just resigned from the job I had since high school in search for a job that paid a little more. He didn't have a job and was always broke, so I had to put up for most of the things we did. It wasn't that much of a big deal to me because I really wanted him off the streets. If I had to front the money for now to keep him off the streets, that was what I would do. I had some savings and was going to interview for a job in a couple of weeks. I know it's usually not wise to leave one job before you have another one, but I knew they weren't going to give me too much time off to go to the medical billing course. The classes were pretty short, so that meant we had to go to classes Monday to Friday, not leaving much time for work. I wanted to focus on the course and was excited that we were going to complete the course together, and he could finally land him a good-paying, decent job. The most convenient thing about taking this class was there was a bus that took us to the school. We just had to take one bus from our house to the downtown area and, from there, take the shuttle bus to the school. It couldn't get any more convenient than that. It left us with more time to just focus on our studies and not worry about how we were going to get back and forth. It was definitely easier on my pockets.

It was different meeting other people together. We were from two different worlds, and we never met each other's friends. Aside from that one hello he said to my girlfriend outside the campus, that was the extent of his interaction with my inner circle. This course was something new; we were starting on the same page. The people at this course were pretty friendly, and the instructors were awesome. He seemed to be picking up so far on a lot of the things they were teaching us. He was definitely smarter than I expected him to be. We enjoyed doing our assignments together and helping each other out. We were given different variations of assignments to do, and some of them required us working with other in teams. It was definitely more women than it was men. We were most of the time put in groups of four in which the class didn't consist of more than about sixteen to twenty people. In the groups, there was always one guy to every three women. He was a comedian, and I hadn't seen that side of him since elementary school. He was getting along really well with the guys, and they would often joke together. It was just a good vibe all the way around. We were getting our education and meeting new people at the same time. Our future was looking very bright until it wasn't.

In my group, there was this guy who was extremely friendly. You know those guys who really mean no harm but can come off a bit flirtatious. Well, with that being said, why oh why did Mr. Flirtatious have to be in my group? My boyfriend and I weren't in the same group, which I thought wasn't a big deal. Apparently, he thought it was to which he asked the instructors to put us in the same group. Unfortunately, the instructors didn't tell him what he wanted to hear, and he began challenging them in why their decision couldn't be changed. It didn't help that during this challenge, Mr. Flirtatious made such a smart comment geared toward the instructor, which led me to burst into laughter. If I could take that moment back, I would. This turned out to be one of the most regretful moments in my life. Who knew this would be the beginning of my first public humiliation? Here to come my first public audience in the most classic ass whooping there is! Who knew that I would ever see the day that he would whoop my ass in public, with no hesitation and no care in the world of any consequences of his actions to follow? It was almost like I made him feel he was invincible and untouchable. After all, I never reported him to the proper authorities. I already let him get away with too much. Remember, we were already past attack number 2, and I was still with him. What do you expect to happen, what message are you sending when a man flat-out balls his fist and punches you in the face, giving you a blow so hard it brings you to your knees and you are still with him?

The class continues, and after the determination of groups not changing, we resumed to our regular scheduled group assignments. When I tell you this guy in my group was funnnnnny, he was funny, you know the Bernie Mac and Katt Williams funny. Even if I tried not to laugh, it was hard for me not to. Each time our table laughed, I would get the death stare from my boyfriend. It got so bad that I just decided to not even look his way anymore. When I did look at him, his legs were moving rapidly up and down as if he was so anxious to leave the class. The class was finally over, and we were all gathering our belongings to go. He rushed toward me and pulled me by my arm. He asked, "What the fuck was so funny? You think that motherfucker is funny? I'll show you funny!" At this point, I was like "Are you serious right now? We are in the middle of a classroom full of people, and you want to make a scene and question me about a fucking guy that I barely even know? You seriously mad because I laughed at his jokes?" He insisted, "I'm not mad because you were laughing at his jokes. It's that fact that you knew he was mocking me." I was hella confused at this point because at no point did this guy even mention or talk about my boyfriend. The entire time he was making fun of the instructor. I tried to explain that to him, but he wouldn't listen. He already had it set in his mind that we were laughing at him, and nothing was going to change his mind.

We were getting along so well almost two weeks into the class courses. Why did he have to show his true identity now? How embarrassing it was for those complete strangers to see him pull on me and talk to me in such a demeaning fashion. I hated him for taking away our peace and happiness unnecessarily. We were now outside, waiting for the bus to take us back to the downtown area. While we were waiting for the bus, he continued to question me about this fucking guy. At that point, I was so over the interrogation I proceeded to walk toward a group in the class that I'd become cordial with. I knew that he wouldn't do anything with them standing right there. We got on the bus, and I immediately sat next to this really tall young lady who always showed me kindness. There was no way I was going to sit on the bus next to him so he could grill me and cause an argument. I tried my best to avoid those types of situations. It annoyed me to my core that he was displaying this behavior, giving them something to talk about. We appeared to have such a loving and secure relationship. We held hands majority of the time and even exchanged kisses. Some of the classmates even commented on how cute of a couple we were. Look how easy it was for him to destroy our image in the blink of an eye. For me, it felt like it was more than just an image; it felt like we were actually developing a normal and healthy relationship.

Sitting apart from him only made matters worse for me. Would you believe his bitch ass sat right behind me and the young lady and began pulling my hair through the seats? The first tug was so hard my hair and head pulled all the way back to the chair. It was so obvious the young lady seated next to me looked in shock, asking me what just happened. I ignored the hair pull and told her that it was just my boyfriend being silly. I stood out of the chair looking back at him and told him to stop playing. He gave me this evil stare with no response and just stared at me. I was pretty terrified; I can't even lie and say that I wasn't. I started regretting the fact that I chose to sit next to the young lady and not him. Who knew this would have made matters worse? I was just simply trying to avoid having an argument on the bus. I sat back down in which the hairpulling continued. The young lady seated next to me was becoming pretty agitated. Each time he pulled my hair, she would appear to get angry. She then questioned me. "I don't understand. Why does he keep pulling your hair? It's not funny, and he needs to stop. It's annoying the shit out of me!" she said loud enough where he could hear every single word that was coming out of her mouth. I was surprised that he remained completely silent and had no rebuttal for her.

We exited the bus, and my intention was to avoid him at all cost. I just wanted to head straight to my dorm and forget this day ever happened. I then remembered that I opted not to take summer classes and therefore not staying on campus at this time. Not to mention I didn't tell my parents or sister that I wasn't taking summer classes in which they all thought I was still on campus. Yes, so you guessed it right, I had the genius idea to agree to staying with him during these brief medical billing courses. It seemed like a great idea at the time. Needless to say, there was, but so far, I could go away from him. Despite the harsh reality of my faith settling in, I decided to continue walking with the young lady toward the bus stop to get home. I knew we were going the same place but figured that he wouldn't do anything with an audience. I was so thankful this young lady had to catch the exact same bus I was catching and just two stops before my stop. We walked and talked as she questioned me about my boyfriend. "Was he just playing?" she asked. "It didn't seem like he was playing. He seems kind of crazy. Why are you with him?" she asked. I tried to smooth things out and told her, "That's just the way we play sometimes."

I thought he had gotten the hint and decided to take a different route home. I got off the bus and never looked back to see if he was behind me or not. Not even minutes after me telling the young lady he was just playing, here he came out of nowhere. He began screaming my name and running up to us from behind. I continued to ignore him as I did on the bus, but this time there wasn't about sixteen to twenty people on the bus. He was enraged at this time because I was ignoring him. He jumped in front of me and stopped me dead in my tracks. He asked me if I was trying to be cute in front of my new friend. I felt a little protected with her standing next to me, and I told him to get out of my face. He pushed me back, causing me to lose balance just a little. As soon as I gained my balance, he followed with one hard smack across my left cheek and completed with another one across my right cheek. The young lady who stood about six feet tall and pretty stocky just jumped right in the middle of what would have been his third smack. She pushed him back as he stumbled and dared him to smack me again. She called him a punk motherfucker and started getting the attention of the crowd passing by. She screamed, "Someone please call the police! This guy just beat the shit out of her!" Before I knew it, we were in front of this building that had an actual security guard right at the window of the building. She pulled me into the building out of harm's way and urged the guard to call the police.

Staring at my reflection in the shiny building full of mirrors, there lay his handprints on each side of my cheek. His handprints were imprinted into my cheeks you would have thought someone painted those handprints. I was in tears and so humiliated by what just happened. Of course, he immediately disappeared during all the commotion. The young lady at that point was my hero. I couldn't believe that she would put herself in harm's way for a complete stranger. She stayed with me until the cops arrived and consoled me the entire time. When she confronted him, I just knew that he was going to either punch her or slap her too. He just told her to mind her fucking business, and that was the extent of it. He actually looked really scared to confront her. The cops finally arrived, but at this point, I was shaken, barely being able to talk. She gave the cops the details of the events. I just had to provide his name and address. I was provided with the complaint number, but with all the shaking and shock, it must have fell out of my hands. The young lady even got off at my stop to make sure that he wasn't there waiting for me. At this point, I didn't know where to go, but I knew that I couldn't go to his house. I did, however, want to get my car because that was where it was parked. I didn't want to go to my family's home because he lived right around the corner. All he would have to do was walk past the house and see my car parked there to know that was where I was. I gave the young lady a hug and thanked her repeatedly for standing up for me how she did. She gave me a hug and told me to call her if I needed her. She also told me that she had a couple of cousins who would happily whoop his ass. I laughed for a second and then thought about it and asked her really. I loved her for her courage and strength and didn't even know her. She had the courage that I needed to stand up to him and walk away. I wanted to be her and have the power she held to put that kind of fear in him.

Contemplating where to go, I was fresh out of ideas. I didn't want too many people knowing my business and definitely didn't want to worry my family. Those handprints looked like they were going to need at least a couple of days to fade away. I was like some loaner on the streets as I paced back and forth from his house to mine. I walked to his house to get my car, and there he stood right in front of my car. It was as if he knew I was coming for it and wanted to be there to make sure he stopped me. I paced the street for hours and finally decided to hide behind the bushes blocks away from the house where he wouldn't be able to see me. I was so tired of pacing back and forth, so I decided to just stay in one place and wait for the opportune time that he would walk away from the car. From the incident that happened with him taking my car without permission, I always made sure I kept my keys on my person or hidden. He had no choice but to just sit on it because he couldn't drive away with it. Finally, two hours had passed, and it looked like he was going back in the house. I waited about two minutes and made a run for it. I knew every second count, and I needed to move as fast as possible. After all this was going to be where I lay my head until I figured out what my next course of action would be. With my heart racing and my feet moving as fast as possible, I finally made it to the car. I was so nervous as I pulled the keys out, they dropped to the floor. All I could think about was him hearing the keys and running back out. I couldn't leave it to chance. I rapidly picked the keys up, opened the door, and sped off with the car. I drove off so fast you could hear the tires screeching.

I pulled onto the street of my campus knowing that I could get a decent night's rest without being interrupted. My back windows were tinted, so it was pretty hard to see me back there. My girlfriend was taking summer classes, and I knew in the morning, I could just buzz her room and take a nice hot shower and get some breakfast. I needed to regroup myself and figure out my next move. I was really enjoying the classes and didn't want to stop going. The next morning, I woke, showered, and had breakfast with my friend. She didn't ask too many questions but knew that I would talk to if I needed to. I decided that I wasn't going to stop going to the classes and was confident that he didn't have the courage to show up the next day. He didn't show up the next day, and the young lady who helped me had so many questions. At this point, I was grateful for help but really didn't want to discuss all the details of my abuse with a total stranger. I was humiliated and didn't want to visit that dreadful moment. It didn't help that she shared the details with some of the classmates, and now they, too, wanted to know if I was OK and had questions. Willingly helping someone in my opinion doesn't give you full access to their entire backstory.

About four days passed, and I'd been sleeping in my car on the street of my campus. However, I learned that my family was out of the house at a certain time, and I could go shower there. I continued with the course and noticed that he still hadn't returned to the class. I was really happy at this time as I was not looking forward to seeing him at all. Now we were into the following week, and who showed up to the class? I ignored him and acted as if he didn't even exist. He appeared to have given up as he made no attempts to communicate with me. I didn't feel comfortable riding the bus, so I decided to drive to the classes despite the fact it was putting a big hole into my savings. I gave the young lady a couple of rides home when I did drive my car to classes. I alternated days because I still had to be mindful not to deplete my savings. The third day of him returning to the class, he didn't say a word and stayed as far away from me as possible. The fourth day, the young lady didn't come to class, and I happened to drive this time to class. Upon leaving the class, I got into my car, and it wouldn't start. He saw that I was having car trouble and took this opportune time to offer assistance. I had no choice and really couldn't afford to decline his help. He was able to get my car started and asked for a ride home in which I provided. He apologized and begged for my forgiveness and swore on his mother this time that he would never hit me again. Wow, he had never sworn on anyone before, so maybe this time it was for real. I took him home, and he invited me to come back home. I was so tired and scared of sleeping in my car I happily accepted his offer.

The fifth day upon his return, my hero had returned to class. We normally sat together and was enjoying the moments he wasn't there. Even upon his first three days, we didn't say one word to each other, and I was giving the young lady occasional rides home. I didn't drive the fifth day, but we did ride the bus and sit together. It was disheartening to get on the bus and walk right past the young lady who put her life at risk to help me with the same guy she was protecting me from. I said hello, and she responded, "Really!" I felt ashamed that I was once again back in communication with him especially after what he did. However, he did acknowledge his wrong and swore this time on his mother he wouldn't do it again. We got to class, and needless to say, she didn't sit by me. We were put in groups and given an assignment to talk in front of the class. The assignment was to give scenarios in keeping patients' records confidential. Well, this young lady stood in front of the class and talked about everything other than a patient. She gave the class an example of exactly what happened to me, explained how she put herself in harm's way, and asked what she should do. She never said my name, but she looked directly at me as she gave her example unrelated to the class. To my surprise, the instructor never stopped her and just allowed her to continue. The instructor did bring to her attention that wasn't the exercise but did answer her question. The instructor advised her that under any circumstances should she or anyone put themselves in a dispute among strangers. He even stated surprisingly they always turn around and defend their abusers. Just help from a far and call the police. She said, "I should have just let him beat her stupid ass."

I felt her anger when she said that. I never took her calling me a stupid ass offensively. I believed that was exactly what I was and wanted to apologize to her for disappointing her. After that moment, she said one last thing to me. "You know he's going to beat your dumb ass again!" I wanted to tell her I was sorry and beg for her forgiveness, but he was standing right next to me. He told her, "I told your fat ass to mind your business." She just shook her head and walked away. Even though she never said my name, the entire class knew that it was us she was referring to. She had mentioned it to some of the classmates, but after this, all the classmates knew about our abusive relationship. After that display of humiliation, I couldn't convince myself to return to that course, and it didn't take much for him to say that he was not going either. What a waste of time, I remember saying to myself, but I couldn't face her anymore. I was ashamed in all that she did for me, and I went right back to him. She was extremely mad, but I know it wasn't out of hate. I really felt that she sincerely believed that one day he would kill me and didn't want to see that as my fate. I will eternally be grateful to that young lady who was such a brave soul.

CHAPTER 10

SEVERAL AUDIENCES
TO FOLLOW

WE WERE STILL in summer and looked like we would be able to enjoy it a little more since we didn't have any more classes. We were just spending all our time together since now I was not even on campus and temporarily staying with him. It had been quite an adjustment living together, especially because he appeared to not like staying home. I didn't like hanging out in the streets, and because of our limited finances, it wasn't that much we could get into. I was really looking forward to us completing the course and him possibly getting a good job in medical billing. Unfortunately, he had a record, and there weren't too many options for someone with a criminal pass. He tried getting employment as he went to several interviews. Unfortunately, none of them called him back. I was very afraid that he would get discouraged and want to make that fast money. Considering the fact that he wasn't staying home a lot and I wasn't going out that much, we would see each other mainly at bedtime. He assured me that he wasn't selling drugs and that he was just hanging out with his friends. After all, these were the guys he grew up with. I guess I could trust that he could occasionally go and visit and not have to actually be engaged in their daily criminal activities. I tired trusting him and giving him the benefit of the doubt.

He started complaining that I wasn't spending enough time with him and was encouraging me to go out with him. I told him that I had no plans on hanging out all day on the streets with his friends. He assured me that they didn't hang out on the streets all the time. There was an occasional bar they went to play pool. I told him that maybe one day I would go with him before the summer was over, but I knew that it wouldn't be an ongoing occurrence. He finally convinced me to go with him to go meet up with a couple of his friends. We went back to the old block that we both grew up at. Most of his friends were still there on that same block, and some of them were pretty funny. I didn't mind going to let loose a little bit and have a couple of laughs and drinks. I'd never hung out with him and any of his friends together, but I knew some from elementary school and in passing. I occasionally would stop to talk in the past on my way home, but it was never lengthy. I was looking forward to this day because this would be something that we were doing together for the first time. He always expressed wanting to do more things together and always said it made him feel closer to me. He said the only part of our relationship that was missing was including each other in associations with our friends. I knew that I didn't want him to meet my college friends because I never thought they would get along. He was from the streets, and other than our minor class experience together, he didn't have much exposure to that of associating with others. He was just too hood, but I definitely wasn't ruling out that possibility completely.

It was a wonderful day today, the weather was nice, and I actually had a job interview today. The job, if I get it, would pay a couple of dollars more than what I was making in my previous job. This would help a lot because I would be able to start as early as the following week. It was also going to be part time, allowing enough time for my studies. The interview was in the morning, and if I got this job, the plans were to go and celebrate with a couple of his friends later in the evening. I really didn't want the first time that I was going to hang out with his friends to be included with the celebration of my new job. However, I wasn't going to make it into a big deal because that was what he wanted. Needless to say, I got the job. I was really excited and couldn't wait to share the awesome news with him. Once I shared the news, he didn't seem as excited as I was, so I was assuming that he was probably tired. I suggested that we take a nap before we head out to meet up with his friends. He hadn't slept much the night before, and I had to get up early to get ready for the interview, not leaving him with enough time to get enough rest. I wanted to believe that his lack of enthusiasm for my new job was out of fatigue. Whatever it was that he was going through, I hoped that he changed his attitude with the quickness. I was five seconds away from telling him I wasn't going to go. Why would I want to hang out with him and his friends for the first time while he was in a funk?

You know when they say never doubt your gut feelings, it's so true. We woke up from our nap, and it was sincerely bothering me how unhappy he appeared to be that I had this new job. I had to call him out on it and ask him why he seemed so unhappy that I got this job. He admitted that he wasn't too happy but only because he was scared; I would meet lots of men. The job I was going to be working was predominantly male-dominated. That was a fact. But I got a job that was going to be paying me more, and I could focus more on school while still making good money. Wouldn't that be what was more important? He agreed that it should be but said that didn't take away from there still being a lot of men. I was pissed off that this would even be the reason why he would be unhappy for something good that just happened for me. Essentially, I felt it was for us as he still hadn't found a job yet. However, why was I even surprised of his insecurities? He knew that he didn't treat me how a real man should and had all right to fear me meeting someone to replace him. Needless to say, we were going back and forth, and he was really trying to convince me that I should understand where he was coming from and possibly look for another job. I was in complete shock and asked him if he had lost his mind. "No matter where I work, there will be other men. I can't control that," I told him. "I'm not going to look for another job," I told him. I also suggested that maybe he should go alone to go hang out with his friends. I was no longer in the mood and definitely didn't want to be around people whom I'd never been around before while he was in a bad mood. He wasn't taking no for an answer and insisted I go. For the sake of arguing, I said OK.

We pulled up to the block, and there were all his friends just hanging out in front of their houses drinking. I told him that I already made it clear I wasn't hanging out in no fucking streets. He led me to believe

D. SAULS

that we were going to the bar, play pool, and have a couple of drinks. I wasn't old enough to drink, but he was. The plan was for him to order drinks and just bring them to the pool table where we all would be hanging out. As I was told, they didn't pay attention to who was drinking, just who was purchasing the drinks. This guy was putting me through so much stress I was looking forward to having a couple of drinks and laughs. It didn't look like that would be the night we were going to have. I immediately suggested that I go home, and maybe one of his friends could drive him home, he could catch the bus, or I would just pick him up in the morning. Just as we were going back and forth, one of his friends chimed in and said, "Let's just go to the bar man. If that's what the lady wants, she should get." He continued with "After all, aren't we here to celebrate her new job anyway?" I was so relieved that he intervened, but the look my boyfriend gave him made me kind of fearful for him. For some reason, most of them feared him ever since elementary school. I always remembered so many giving him so much respect and never challenging him much. Either way, I was thankful that my half-ass celebration wasn't going to have to be in the streets.

When we got to the destination, which was literally a short walk up the street, I was surprised at how entertaining the spot looked. They had music playing and several pool tables. I didn't know how to play pool, but I always enjoyed watching others play. He and his friends played as I just pulled up a chair not too far from him and watched him play. It was fun watching him and his friends go back and forth with sarcasm. He was going back and forth from the bar to the pool table. He bought some drinks back for me, but I didn't want to drink that much, especially since I was the one driving us home. I watched as him and his friends drink nonstop. I even suggested to him that he slow down a little bit, but at this point, it was already a little too late. Regardless of his drinking, we were having a lot of fun. His friends were just as funny as I remembered him to be, and it was just nothing but laughs and several cheers to my new job. He went back and forth from the pool table to me and just giving me so many kisses. I was impressed by his display of affection as he maintained such a fun attitude the entire night. We closed the place down! It was about one in the morning, and we needed to go. Lights were being shut, and chairs were being put up. At this point, everyone aside from me was drunk out of their fucking minds. My boyfriend was stumbling as he held on to my shoulders while we exited the bar. Everyone just said bye as they walked home, for they lived minutes away from the bar. The one friend who suggested we go to the bar lived a little bit farther. He asked if he could get a ride home, and I said of course. He said, "Thank you. You're so nice and pretty. What are you doing with this ugly motherfucker?" I burst out in laughter as I thought it was pretty hilarious.

My heart once again dropped to my stomach. The death stare he gave his friend was unbelievable. Mind you, everyone at this point was just piss drunk. He turned around and asked his friend, "What the fuck did you just say?" His friend told him, "Chill, that's a compliment. Your girl is pretty as fuck." He became even more irate and asked his friend, "Why the fuck you are checking out my girl like that?" I chimed in and attempted to come to his friend's defense. I said, "Babe, he's just messing with you. It's not that!" Before I could get the word "serious" out my mouth, he slapped it right back in. He slapped the shit out of my mouth and told me to shut the fuck up. Meanwhile, his friend was sitting right in the back seat. His friend was completely shocked. His friend screamed, "Yo, man, what the fuck you are doing! That's not OK! You a fucking punk for hitting her like that!" Of course, after that smack to the mouth, I was forced to pull the car over. He and his friend continued to argue back and forth, but surprisingly, he never attempted to fight his friend. His friend was pissed and continued to challenge him, telling my boyfriend to get the fuck out the car. They both proceeded out the car, and his friend challenged him to a fight. My boyfriend was hesitant to fight his friend but had no problem with smacking the shit out of me in front of him. They circled for a good ten minutes with their hands up, but no blows were exchanged. He continued to plea with his friend and told him to just mind his fucking business. He said, "We boys from since we were little. How you going to let how I deal with my bitch get in the middle of that?" Surprisingly, his boy said, "No, man, she not a bitch. You are for hitting her." I couldn't believe that once again, someone was putting their selves out there for me. I yelled to his friend, "It's OK. Just let me take you home. Stop going back and forth with him. It's almost two in morning now, and we are making all this noise in the streets. Someone is bound to call the cops, and you both going to end up in jail."

At this point, his friend and I were just coming to the defense of each other. I was telling him it was not worth it, and he was telling my boyfriend to fight a fucking man, not a woman. At this point, my boyfriend became completely confused on why his boy was protecting me like this. Not surprisingly, the next thing that came out of his mouth was if we were fucking. Mind you, up until this night, I'd never even uttered words other than hello to this guy. I knew nothing about him other than he was a friend of my boyfriend. His friend told him how stupid he sounded and continued to put his hands up, challenging my boyfriend to a fight. At this point, I'd exhausted all possible ways to get them to stop arguing and get in the car. His friend approached him and took a swing at him, missing. He countered punches with a right and left hook in which both landed. Needless to say, his friend was knocked out cold on the floor with just those two punches. It was crazy seeing the strength of his hits on someone else. He was so powerful, and he knew that. That was why he kept telling his friend to leave it alone because he knew what he was capable of. How could he use those deadly weapons to harm me like this, knowing the strength in those hands of his? Now his poor friend was laid out cold on the floor, and they both were still fucking drunk.

He felt so bad as he leaned down to his friend, trying to get him to wake up. I felt horrible that he was laid on the floor trying to protect me. I went toward him as well and just started blowing on his face and putting water on it from the bottle of water that was in my car. Thankfully, his friend woke up and was still pissed. He continued to argue with my boyfriend while he was a distance away. At this point, I ran my hands across his face and begged him to leave it alone. Tears were running down my face, and my boyfriend was pacing back and forth. He continued to mumble, "I told him to mind his business. I told him I didn't want to fight him. Why he couldn't just mind his business?" He stopped mumbling to himself, realizing that his friend was now awake. He breathed a sigh of relief as he ran to hug his friend. "I'm sorry, man. I'm really sorry. Now let's just get you home." His friend insisted that he was not getting in the car and would just walk home. Now he was completely drunk and just got knocked the fuck out. It was about three in the morning now and would probably take hours for a taxi to come. There was no way that I was going to leave him out here alone. If I didn't do anything else for him, the least I could do was make sure he got home. Finally, after his friend saw that I wasn't leaving no matter what he said, he agreed to let us take him home. We got to his house, and my boyfriend attempted to help him to the door. He reluctantly declined the help but later realized that he had no choice. He could barely walk and couldn't even find the keys to his house, which were right there in his pocket. He had no choice but to accept the help in which my boyfriend walked him all the way to his bedroom. I had all intentions of driving off and leaving him there but knew the outcome of his anger wouldn't be worth it. It was becoming apparent to me that he didn't care who the audience was. He was becoming comfortable to hit me in front of his actual friends. Strangers and now friends, who else would be next?

He got in the car, and there was complete silence. You could tell that he was completely exhausted and just wanted to sleep away the alcohol. I stayed quiet and definitely had nothing to say to him. Well, actually I had a lot of things to say to him. I wanted to tell him how fucked he was for fucking his friend up like that. How fucked he was for calling me a bitch in front of his friend. How especially fucked up it was that he just freely slapped me in the mouth in front of his friend. I knew that this probably wouldn't be the best time. We were minutes away from home, and he just burst out into tears. "I'm really sorry that this happened. I feel horrible," he told me, "and really tried my best for this not to happen again. I was drinking a lot, and it clouded my judgment. Did you see how he was just disrespecting me like that flirting with you? You sure you and him not fucking? I saw how you was rubbing his face with the water." I asked him where he got his nerve from. "You know that I don't know him like that! You knocked him the fuck out, and I was making sure that you didn't fucking kill him! You lucky that rubbing his face was all I needed to do to get him to wake up!" He stopped and thought for a minute and realized how stupid he sounded. "I just have to work on not drinking like this. You see, the only time this happens is when I drink a lot." In which that was a complete lie because remember, he kicked my ass in broad day light. We had just come from class, and he wasn't drinking. But I listened to him, remaining quiet. I knew better than to challenge him, especially after that beating I just saw him give his friend. I could only imagine that my faith would be ten times worse.

At this point, I knew that whatever love feelings I had for him completely went out the door after witnessing him beat his friend like that. I can still feel the slap he gave me and can't unsee the ass whooping he gave his friend. Who was this guy? How dangerous was he? I remember thinking. How am I going to get myself out of this one? Every moment I spent with him, I dreaded. If I was a little scared before, that scene made me deathly afraid of him. I wanted to leave but felt trapped. He was so possessive and violent I didn't see myself leaving peacefully. I was literally sleeping with my biggest enemy. Days went by, and I was still traumatized from that scene. I lay in the bed for days as he attempted to talk to me. I was so mentally drained that I had no words for him. It felt like my soul had left my body. I just cried for days and barely had an appetite. I wanted to go home but knew that I didn't want to draw him to my family's house. I knew if I left, that would be the first place he would look for me. I needed an escape plan but didn't have one. Every time he got near me to see how I was doing, I would just cringe. My cries would get louder as I would beg him to get away from me. Almost one week went by, and I was still barely eating or getting out the bed to shower. At this point, I could actually start to smell myself but didn't have the strength to do anything for myself.

He was such in panic mode and didn't know how to deal with my silence. We were literally in the same bed, and my mental couldn't grasp talking to him. I had nothing to say to him, and the more he tried talking to me, the more I would shut down. He finally decided to just leave me alone and let me be for one day. He knew there was nothing that he could do that would undo what I saw him do. He was a monster to me and definitely something to be very afraid of. After that one day, he brought the phone to me the next day. "Someone wants to talk to you," he said. At this point, I knew that there was no possible person that he could put me on the phone with that I would want to talk to. I asked him who it was, and he didn't want to tell me. I declined to talk to the person and asked him to leave me alone. He insisted that I take the phone and forcefully put it to my ears. He had a female cousin who he was really close with and always wanted us to meet. The only side of his family I knew was his grandmother and three siblings. Aside from that, I haven't met anyone else. With the phone finally to my ear, I heard a soothing voice, saying, "Hey, sweetie, I heard you not feeling well and haven't been eating. I'm going to have him bring you over so we can fix you all up." I told her I didn't feel like driving and that he didn't have his license and couldn't drive. She offered to come and pick us up in which I didn't expect that. I wondered if he told her exactly what happened and why I wasn't feeling well. After several minutes on the phone, she finally convinced me to come. I told her I wasn't coming today but maybe tomorrow. It felt good that I was at least going to meet another side of his family. I was sure it took a lot for her to even ask me to come, never meeting me at all. I didn't want to seem rude and accepted her invitation. After all, he would always brag about this cousin and how much fun he would have with her.

The next day, we were getting ready to go to his cousin's house, but I still didn't have much to say to him. The drive was about twenty to thirty minutes from his house. We finally arrived, and we were greeted by his cousin waiting outside for us. She proceeded to me and gave me the biggest hug. "It's so nice to meet you. You're actually the first girlfriend he ever bought to the house. You are definitely special," she told me. "There's a change of plans," she told me. "We're going to go to our great-grandmother's house instead. She cooked up a wonderful meal, and there are several family members waiting to meet you." Now I was starting to feel really special that they were doing all this for me. We walked into his great-grandmother's house, and there was this big spread of food. I wanted to say that they had to have already planned this, and I was just included in it. There was no way they did this for me. He and his cousin led me to believe it was all for me, but I never believed that. Why would you go all out like this for a girlfriend that you never met? It was not like we were engaged or anything. Needless to say, I still felt the gesture was heartfelt, and it definitely took me out of that PTSD I was having for the past week.

I have to say everyone was so nice and friendly. I met almost the majority of his cousins from young to old. They played a lot of cards and board games. I learned how to play Pokeno for the first time, which was almost like bingo. It was a lot of fun. I do have to say that his family did a lot of drinking and smoking cigarettes though. Well, needless to say, one of his cousins offered me a cigarette as I was outside getting some fresh air. His cousin was a little bit younger than him and seemed to have his head on a little straighter than my boyfriend. He had an actual job! He told me that his cousin had never brought any girl to the house, so this was new for all of them. He said, "You don't even seem like his type because you're so pretty and nice." He said the whole family was shocked when you walked through the door. "You're definitely special," his cousin said. "I know what he does, and you just don't seem like a girl that would be around that."

I was completely thrown back by how up front his cousin was and was sharing a whole lot with me. I told him that he doesn't do that anymore. He chuckled and said, "OK, well, for your sake, I hope so." He definitely had me thinking about the possibilities that he was still doing that. I wanted to ask him more questions but started to get a little worried that we were out here way too long. I didn't know where he was at exactly but knew that he wasn't far away. I wanted to get back to his great-grandmother's before he noticed that I was gone. His cousin sure did have a lot of info to tell and appeared to want to give me the entire box of tea. I had to decline as I didn't want what happened to his friend to happen to his cousin. I don't believe they knew that side of him or what he was capable of. I wanted to spare them from that. I was really enjoying my time with them as it was actually making what we had felt normal again. He was a different person around his family. I went back upstairs and found him at the table playing cards. He asked where I was at, and I told him I was just out getting some fresh air. He got up, pulled a chair closer to him, gave me a kiss on the lips, and said, "Stay close to me, baby." It worked again; he took me out of that hating him stance. I was back to liking him as he made me feel really good that he wanted me to meet his family. You know it's always a big deal for anyone to meet their significant other's family.

Needless to say, a month went by, and this had now become our new thing to do. It was perfect because we didn't have that much money. His family always cooked and played games. I knew that we would always be in for some good laughs, food, and drinks. He was always well behaved in front of them, until he wasn't. This particular day, everything started off pretty calm as it usually did. We were having so much fun, and it was never a dull moment. We mainly spent time at his great-grandmother's place, as it seemed that was where everybody would go. His cousin, I believe, lived in the same building or the next one over. It was always close to go from one apartment to the next. He was playing his usual card games, which I now discovered was for money. Now it made sense why he would be so glued to that table. While he was glued to the table, I went out to have a cigarette. His cousin was out there and we began talking for a while. I realized I was gone for quite some time and he would probably be looking for me. I immediately returned back. He asked me why was I gone so long and who was I smoking with? Of course, he had been drinking and continued to loudly interrogate me in front of his entire family. His great-grandmother began to yell at him, asking him what the big deal was when he also smoked. She continued to tell him that I was not his child, and he shouldn't be talking to me like that.

Of course, now he realized that he was bringing attention to himself. Mind you, he'd never been around his family like at this magnitude, so I didn't know this side of him. He was embarrassed and told me to come outside with him. He apologized to the family, grabbed his money, and said, "Let's go." I was hesitant to leave as he threatened to humiliate me in front of his family. I didn't think that he would go to that extreme, but I definitely didn't want to disrespect their home with this kind of nonsense. We proceeded to go downstairs as he was pushing me down the stairs. I began to walk faster, realizing that he was trying to cause me to fall down the stairs. I ran outside to get to the car, and he couldn't even wait. He punched me in the back of my head, and I yelled out for him to stop. He continued pulling my hair and now punching me in the stomach. He told me how I'd been completely disrespectful, causing him to be humiliated in front of his family. I was screaming for him to stop as the hits just kept coming. His great-grandmother heard my screams. She continued to yell through the window for him to stop hitting me and urged for me to come back upstairs. She screamed for the cousins to come down and help me, but at this point, it was too late. He pulled me by my hair and dragged me into the car. I didn't have the energy to fight, and I didn't want them to get involved. I didn't know if he would try to hurt them too. I didn't think that he would do anything to his great-grandmother but didn't know if he would try and fight his younger cousins. In my eyes, it didn't matter if they were male or female; anyone could get it. I saw his punching power and have felt them more than I wanted to. I didn't want anyone else subjected to that. I could have fought him off a little longer until they reached downstairs, but I didn't want that on my conscience.

It was becoming the norm for him to have so many audiences to follow as he displayed his anger toward me. I used to think that there was a limit to what he would and wouldn't do in front of people. Apparently, he was starting to feel invincible. He was hitting me in front of strangers, friends, and now family members. There were no consequences for him as I let him get away with it each time. I never called the cops on him. The only time the cops were called was when that young lady put herself in harm's way to protect me. I always threatened to call the cops on him but was so worried of the trouble he would get into if I called the cops on him. I didn't want to be the reason he was going to jail. As crazy as it sounds, I wanted to protect him from that. I kept going back to him each time. How stupid would I look if I now got the cops involved and still went back to him? So many reasons for me to protect him it was no wonder why he was spiraling out of control. He was beating me so much now that he stopped apologizing. Every attempt of me leaving would be followed by a threat to kill me. "Where do you think you going? Do you really think I'm going to let you walk away like that? You're mine forever!"

CHAPTER 11

FIRST HOSPITAL VISIT

THE SUMMER WAS almost over, and it had been nothing shy of humiliations and beatings. I couldn't wait to go back to campus and far away from him as possible. I turned him into a monster that had no remorse for his actions, nor did he fear any repercussions from his actions. I had lost so much of my self-esteem I began making sure that I was on my best behavior. I began feeling like these beatings were my fault. I would talk back a lot. Maybe I just needed to learn how to shut up. I was mindful of my words, actions, and interactions with the opposite sex because anything seemed to set him off. It was about two weeks before I went back to school and counting down the days. I used to couldn't wait to be with him; now I was counting down the days to get as far away from him as possible. I tried to do the rest of my time there quietly. I would talk less and decline any opportunity to go out with him. I never really used to ask where he was going but was happy each time he left and came back really late. I hated him and wanted him gone out of my life. I hated the very sight, touch, and smell of him. He was bitch in a man's body. He would always direct all his anger toward me and hesitate with others. I would often wonder, what did I do to deserve such a man? He started out as my biggest crush and turned out to be my biggest nightmare.

The day had finally come, and I was back on campus. It felt like I just got released from jail. I felt so free and safe. I didn't have to watch what I say and who I talked to in fear of getting a beatdown. I just wanted to focus on getting back my mental so I could do good in these up and coming classes. He wanted me to actually stay with him and not go back on campus. I told him that was definitely not happening. Of course, we argued about that up until the day I left. He was so fucking stupid he didn't understand the process of enrollment. I already enrolled and paid my money to stay on campus. It was very expensive to live on campus, so why would I not go? "There is no benefit in me staying with you," I told him. "All I am is your punching bag, and I choose not to be that." I had no intentions on staying in contact with him, but of course, I didn't let him know that. The plan was to just ignore him as much as possible. I would hope that he would feel shameful enough from all the beatings to leave me alone. I knew it was only a matter of time before he came looking for me. I was always hopeful however that one day he would just give up. A whole lot of wishful thinking that was on my part!

It was going really good in my eyes. Months went by, and there was no sign of him. I was getting really excited until I remembered that was the norm for him. He had gone months before where we would not communicate at all, and out of the blue, he would show up. I told my dorm mate/ girlfriend about the sparring match I was in with him the whole summer. We were talking a lot more, and I really felt good being able to let someone in on what was going on with me. Something like that no human being can go through without having some sort of outlet. She had become my outlet. She would always question why I was still in that situation but never made me feel judged. She would always tell me in due time when I had enough, I would know when to leave. She would always express a hope that he didn't kill me first. Despite the fact that I was very private, she really made me feel like I could trust her with that. I would always urge her to keep my business private. She told me that this wasn't just my business; it was everyone's. She also told me that the bruises on my face that I thought no one noticed, well, they did. Apparently, while I was away for the summer, I became the topic of conversation. I didn't talk personal with anyone but her. She told me how everyone was coming to her asking her if I was in an abusive relationship. I always had a different bruise every other week. I was so surprised to hear that as I thought I was hiding them very well. You never know who's watching and observing what.

OK, we are going on the third month now and still nothing from him. I really thought I was in the clear. I don't remember that much time going buy without him trying to find some way to reconnect. My girlfriend and I took one class together this semester. We had different majors, so it was but so many classes we could take alike. Well, we were walking to our class, joking and laughing as usual. This girl was the female version of Bernie Mac. When I say she was funny, she was really funny. In the midst of laughter, I heard "Oh shit, there he is." I looked up, and he was walking toward us. I knew it was too good to be true, but it was good while it lasted. I continued walking toward him and had no intentions on stopping. We started walking faster, and he quickly turned around to go in our direction. I forcefully asked him why he was here. He asked if he could talk to me for a second, and my girlfriend quickly interrupted and said, "No, we have to go to class., He looked at her with this evil smirk on his face and ignored her. He asked the question again, and I reiterated what she just said. "We're late for class," I told him, "and don't have time to talk." He said, "Well, I'll just wait for you until you're done." I told him I had several more classes after that and not to wait for me. Finally getting away from him, my girlfriend asked if I had lost my mind letting that skinny motherfucker beat on me like that. "He looks hungry," she said. "Just hide his food, and he won't have no strength to beat you. If he tries, you could just push him over." I was dying with laughter but still in the back of my mind knew he would be waiting for me until whatever time I got out of class.

I couldn't believe how frail and hungry he looked. He had this oversized T-shirt and jacket. He was already small in stature and always had an athletic physique. Today he just looked like a hungry homeless man. I tried not to think too much about the way he looked as I started to feel sorry for him. I wondered why he was looking like that and was hoping he was OK. I really hoped that he wasn't there when I got out. I wouldn't have my girlfriend with me because she would be in a whole different class. I knew all he would have to do was get my ear, and I would take him back with open arms. I was a sucker for people's bad situations. Even though he became my abuser, I always tried to hold on to that guy I fell in love with. That guy I always cared about and wanted nothing bad to happen to him. The guy who started off shielding me from evil just to later become my evil I needed shielding from. I had such a loving heart and never wanted to see people suffering or in pain.

It didn't register for me that I was suffering the most at the hands of this man whom I was so concerned about. What had I become where I was more worried about my abuser than myself? I really prayed for God to harden my heart. I knew this guy didn't deserve any of my time or energy but would somehow manage to suck it out of me. It was going to happen one way or the other. It was so unavoidable, and I was so angry with myself for being so weak. I wanted so bad for him to release the hold he had on me, but it was so hard.

Of course, by the time I got to class, I hung around as long as possible. If he was out there, I assumed that he would eventually get tired. I didn't expect him to know where my classes where because they were in different parts of the campus. The campus was pretty big, and thankfully for me, you couldn't get into the library without your student ID. It had been about three hours since I saw him, and I stayed about forty-five minutes after my class was over, just going over some homework. Unfortunately, another class would be starting in another fifteen minutes, and I would have to vacate the classroom. I slowly peeped my head out the window, making sure he was nowhere in sight. He could come into buildings where the classes were being held, and I wasn't sure to what level he was determined to speak to me. Finally making sure the coast was clear, I rapidly made my way to the library. I remained there for the rest of the evening until I got tired. I figured by now, four hours had passed since I saw him last, there was no way he would still be there waiting for me. I was making my way to the dorms, and it was getting pretty dark. I began walking in fear as I had no idea where he was. I finally made it to the front of my dorm, breathing a sigh of relief. Just as I took my last breath to exhale, I saw him coming out of the bushes like some fucking psychotic stalker. He startled me so bad I almost fell into the bushes.

"What the fuck do you want? Why are you bothering me? Please leave me alone," I begged him. His eyes began to tear up as he told me he'd been sleeping at friend's houses. I looked at him in complete disbelief as he had that mansion he shared with his grandmother. "How could you possibly be homeless?" I asked. He told me he and his grandmother had an argument, and she was making it uncomfortable for him to be there. "That sounds so stupid. So what if you guys are arguing? Just ignore her. Why would that be a reason for you to not go home?" He proceeded to tell me that she found out from the family how he'd been abusing me and was harassing him about it. I suggested that he just go back home and figure it out. He began to walk away but sobbing at the same time. He knew that would get me. Fortunately for him, my roommate was never in our shared room, so I had the room to myself. I invited him to stay but only for a couple of days. It was against my better judgment, but he led me to believe his next stop would be sleeping in the streets. My heart couldn't handle the thought of that. We went upstairs, and as soon as I opened the door, my dorm mates were all in the living room. I said hello to everyone and walked right straight to my room, not introducing him to no one.

My girlfriend was pissed and walked right into my room. "Why the fuck is he here?" She knew exactly how not to bite her tongue. It didn't even matter to her that he was sitting right there. Of course, like the punk he was, he remained silent. It was becoming apparent that he only had that harmful energy for me. At this juncture, I didn't like how she was yelling or talking to me. "I appreciate your concern," I told her, "but I don't answer to you." I asked her to leave as I kindly shut and locked the door upon her immediate exit. My heart was so sad as I felt like I might have just lost the only friend whom I was able to share my terrors with. Unfortunately, that was the price I was willing to pay to avoid him sleeping in the streets as he led me to believe that would be his outcome. He was so pitiful-looking and so humble. He began kissing me and thanking me so much for sticking up for him. The night passed, and he wouldn't leave me alone. He just kept feeling me up the whole night, wanting to have sex. Just the thought of him touching me repulsed me. I pushed him off a couple of times, but he just kept trying. The more I pushed him, the louder he would be insisting I was with somebody else. I didn't want to make a scene or any noise, so I just gave up fighting and let him do whatever he wanted to me. I did let him know the next day that this wasn't going to be ongoing. I told him the only reason why it happened was because I didn't want to make a scene. "If you continue to touch me and demand sex, I will just have to end your visit short." He looked at me with such confusion but knew he had no choice but to agree. I tried to respect everyone's privacy and only came out with him when I knew that all my dorm mates were gone. I had him shower and brush his teeth, especially it was all women there. He had to leave when I left and figure out what he was going to do for the time I was in school. I definitely wasn't leaving him alone in my room. He had no choice but to comply as I reminded him that his days were being numbered, and he needed to resolve things at home immediately so he could leave. His mood had definitely softened as he seemed so sad. He lacked any type of energy and genuinely appeared to be happy he had a place to lay his head.

Just as I was thinking to give him a couple more days, I had an intervention. All my dormmates came to me and told me that they no longer wanted him there and that he needed to leave, or they would report me. I was confused because all of us had overnight visitors, and some had guest who stayed longer than the three days he had been there already. I made sure he was never left in the room without me, and they barely saw him. I asked them what their problem was and told them if they reported me, they might as well report themselves too. I was starting to suspect that my girlfriend told them who he was, and that was why they were pressuring him to leave. I didn't want him there as much as they didn't want him but definitely wasn't going to let them intimidate me when they were doing the exact same thing. I could see if we argued in front of them, but we didn't. He would legit just meet up with me when I was done with my classes, get some food, and come to my room and sleep. This was the quietest I'd seen him aside from the first night. However, I did need him to leave and was going to give him a couple more days.

He told me that he needed to just let his grandmother calm down before he could go back to the house. He also said that he was tired of sleeping on friends' couches and didn't want to spend the little money he had on hotels. He asked me if he could stay another week, and I told him hell no. "You have a couple more days, and that's it." I let him know that my dorm mates weren't comfortable with him there and that I could get in trouble. Of course, he could care less about that. He had no choice but to understand that was what it was. He seemed to understand as the last day, he began to gather his belongings. On the day he was supposed to leave, we just happened to have a living room full of male company. He saw that and decided that he wasn't leaving today. It didn't matter that they weren't my company; he was just intimidated by their presence. I insisted that he didn't make a scene and walked ahead of him to the elevator. I needed him to follow me and keep him away from my dorm. There were lots of people there, and I really didn't want him to make a scene and humiliate me for the hundredth time. We were arguing on the elevator, and he began to shove me. I told him to stop before I called the fucking cops this time. He accused me of wanting him to leave so I could be with one of those guys upstairs. He said, "Now I see why you didn't want to give me any pussy!" We were going back and forth shouting over each other. I told him even if one of those guys were for me, it was none of his fucking business. "I only let you stay out of fucking pity. Why do you think I didn't even want you fucking touch me? Now please fucking leave, and don't come back. I don't give a fuck where you sleep at tonight or the next."

We finally got to the first floor, and he brought the elevator back to my floor. Blood just started pouring from my mouth. I fell to my knees from the hard impact of his balled-up fist to my mouth, followed by the kick with his hard timberlands to my stomach. After I extended myself to help this motherfucker, he was kicking me like a fucking animal. I didn't even see it coming. It happened so fast as I was fighting to get off the elevator, and he was trying to pull me back in. I began yelling as best as I could and kicking him away from me as I was still on the floor. Thankfully, someone yelled, "What's going on?" and that immediately scared him away. I crawled to my dorm room that wasn't far from the elevator. My hands were full of blood, and it was at this point pouring from my mouth. I grabbed the handle to the door, leaving it with my bloody handprints, barely screaming for help. These strange men in my dorm room immediately ran out the room, looking for him. I passed out for a second and woke up to the ambulance and campus police. They were asking me what happened, but I could barely speak. Just to realize that he punched me so hard my teeth split right through the right cheek of my mouth, getting stuck. That was where all the blood was coming from. The police had to get descriptions from my dorm mates and girlfriend. As I sat with my body and clothes covered with blood, my girlfriend was crying and consoling me. As the police took pictures of my bruises, she stayed right by my side and told the police all that she knew. She definitely was the definition of a good friend.

Fortunately for me, there was a hospital right next to the campus. I don't remember how I got to the hospital as my memory faded in out a lot after those brutal attacks. I do remember my girlfriend accompanying me to the emergency room and explaining for me to the nurses what happened. They had to cut the inside of my lip to release the connection it had to my teeth. I had to get close to twenty-six stiches that night. I was so worried that they wouldn't find him. Once I got released from the hospital, my girlfriend was right there waiting for me, with those guys who went looking for him. I thanked them for their bravery and their extended concern in wanting to make sure I got home safe. I was relieved to find out that they did catch him, and of course, he denied ever being there or knowing me. He told them they had the wrong guy and that he was just passing through. Thankfully, all my dorm mates were able to give a positive ID of the asshole. I got to my room in tears and completely ashamed of what happened to me. The dorm mates whom I barely talked to now knew my most private humiliation. Even if they weren't sure before, he solidified their doubts. I was balled up on my bed as they all came in, hugged me, and asked me if I was OK. You can tell that they genuinely cared and wasn't being nosy. They described it as a scene from a horror movie, and the thought of that made me cringe. They weren't too intrusive as they didn't stay long in my room. My girlfriend stayed with me a little until I told her I just wanted to be alone. She asked me if she should call my sister, and I told her that was the last thing I wanted her to do. My sister would have died knowing that happened to me, and I wanted to shield her from that kind of hurt. She respected my wishes and just let me be but not before giving me a big hug, followed by a bursting of tears. "I'm so glad you're OK, and please let me know if you need anything as I'm right next door," she reminded me.

One week went by, and I hadn't been to class. My face was pretty bruised up. The doctor had given me a note, excusing me from my classes for one week. My job was going pretty well, and I had built a very good rapport with the managers. They knew I was going to school, and thankfully, I was part time. I was able to get some time off for school without having to tell them the details of my abuse. I just stayed in my room and only got up to shower when everyone left. I had a little mini fridge and got enough food to last for one week. I didn't want to come out that room for nothing. The hospital also had a social worker follow up with me to make sure I was OK and direct me to resources that could help women like me. Of course, it went through one ear and out the other as I wasn't ready to accept that kind of help. I also got a visit from the campus police following up with me to make sure I was OK. A couple of hours later, I got a visit from some detectives. I was confused by the overwhelming concern. I just got a visit from the campus police and now detectives. Why were detectives questioning me? They were asking me questions that didn't have to do with my well-being and everything to do with my abuser. When they saw my confusion with these questions, they later told me that he was apprehended with a large number of narcotics on his person. My heart dropped, and I couldn't believe that he brought that shit to my school. They wanted to know if I had anything to do with the drugs or knew about it. My heart was beating so fast as I became extremely nervous with the questioning. I knew they couldn't possibly think that I had something to do with that. I knew nothing about it and became agitated that they were interrogating me like I did. I answered their questions to the best of my ability and told them I was done answering questions. I was advised that they would be reaching out to me if they had any further questions.

The next day, my girlfriend came to check on me, and I told her what happened with the detectives. She advised me that the detectives had been by the room and questioned everyone in our dorm apartment. They even got the information of those guys who helped me out and questioned them too. I couldn't believe they were really looking into me as being part of his drug connection. I was terrified that I would even be associated with something like that. He really could give two shits about me bringing this to my school, and now I was under investigation for something I knew nothing about. I was terrified and wondering if I was going to have to get a lawyer. Just as I felt like my entire world was about to be destroyed, I got a phone call from the campus police. This was the guy who actually caught my abuser. I would always see him around making sure that everyone was OK. He was always so friendly, respectful, and courteous to us all. He asked if we could schedule a time to meet, and I told him maybe next week because my face was still pretty bruised up. He told me it couldn't wait until next week and would have to be as soon as possible. It made me really nervous when he said that, so I asked him if we could meet in a couple of hours.

We met up at the campus diner. Of course, I was all disguised with my hat, shades, and scarf wrapped around my mouth. There he stood looking really concerned for me. I was thinking, *Are they investigating me too?* Once I reached him, I was greeted by a big hug. He became tearful, and I was in complete shock at this moment. I only knew this man from seeing him on campus, and here he was crying for me. I began tearing, and he was apologizing for his tears. We both gathered our composure enough for me to ask him why I was here. He asked me if I believe in God, and I told him that I do. He told me that he had never seen such a beautiful woman beaten so bad. He told me the image of my busted lip and bloodied clothes haunted him in his sleep. He wanted to tell me to love myself enough to let this be the last time I ever dealt with this monster. He also told me that the investigation on me was over and that I could have been expelled and possibly charged with intent to distribute on school grounds. He told me that thankfully for me, everyone that they interviewed was very animate of me not being involved. They even went as far as giving sworn written testimonies suggested by my girlfriend. "This man nearly took your life twice. He could have killed you, or you could have been in jail! No one's worth that. You're somebody's daughter, sister, and friend. I'm sure they want to see you alive for years to come. I needed to tell you this so I can sleep better at night." I was so relieved with the news he delivered but so ashamed that he even had to see me this way. I thanked him for his gratitude and gave him the biggest hug. As we were hugging, he whispered in my ear, "You're so much better than that. Love yourself and move on. I better not ever see you on campus with this guy again." I hugged him once again and assured him that would never be the case. I was so thankful that this stranger took the time out of his busy life to give me those words of wisdom. I really didn't want to disappoint him or any of them who stuck their necks out for me.

CHAPTER 12

IRREVERSIBLE

I WAS THANKFUL THAT he was arrested, but I was also fearful that he would still come looking for me, even more so now that he got arrested, and his drugs were confiscated. I was humiliated and embarrassed that everyone on campus seemed to know about what happened to me. It just felt like everywhere I turned, someone was looking at me. I wasn't able to focus on school like I should and didn't want to be there anymore. All my dreams and aspirations felt like they had been shattered. I was living in fear and was terrified that he would come and do worse harm to me. I needed to finish this semester out, and I was going to withdraw from school. I began doing extra hours at work while still trying to close this semester out with descent grades. I wasn't sure if I was going to let my family know about the assault or the fact that I was going to take a break from school. I was planning on getting my own apartment to gather my thoughts and be by myself for a little. I haven't heard from him and didn't know what his faith was. I didn't know if he was still in jail or home. I only wanted to know that so I could know how to move on the outside. Home wasn't an option for me because he knew where I lived. I always tried to keep that bullshit away from my family. I always came up with some excuse not to come home and visit. As far as they knew, I was really focused on school, and it was keeping me pretty busy. My sister also attending school herself had her own life to focus on, leaving her with less time to worry about me. It was better that way because I knew if she knew half of what was going on with me, she definitely wouldn't have been able to focus on school like she should have.

About a month went by, and I still had a couple of months to go before I could finish out the semester. I had to complete a form for the withdrawal process, and they weren't making it easy. I didn't want to disclose what happened, but I had to tell them I was in fear for my life and give in details the accounts of my assault. I was finally given the approval to withdraw from school and began searching for apartments immediately. It was exhausting and very discouraging to see how expensive it would be for me to live on my own. The end of my semester, I was feeling very tired and nauseous. I would go to work and always have to leave early because I wasn't feeling well. I would get the overtime and wouldn't even be able to work them. One of my coworkers said to me, "Congratulations! You're glowing." I asked her to further explain as I had no idea what she was talking about. She began laughing and asked me how many months I was. I was completely confused and scared of the thought that I might be pregnant. She was an older lady and insisted that I was pregnant. She said, "Sweetheart, why do you think you keep going to the bathroom every five minutes and leaving work early all the time. I'm pretty sure that you are, but just go to the doctor and get yourself checked out." That was the last thing I needed, to be pregnant with his child and living on my own. Why was this happening to me? I finally felt like he was completely out of my life, and now I might be carrying his child. What did I do to deserve such a horrible fate? I've imagined having children with him during the honeymoon stage of our relationship. The imagination quickly disappeared when he became abusive. I knew the baby was innocent and a blessing, but he wasn't.

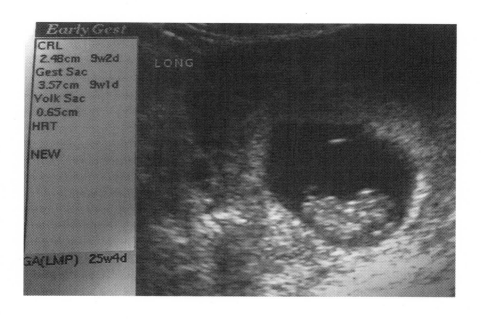

CRL
 2.48cm 9w2d
Gest Sac
 3.57cm 9w1d
Yolk Sac
 0.65cm
HRT

NEW

LONG

Early Gest

GA(LMP) 25w4d

BEATEN

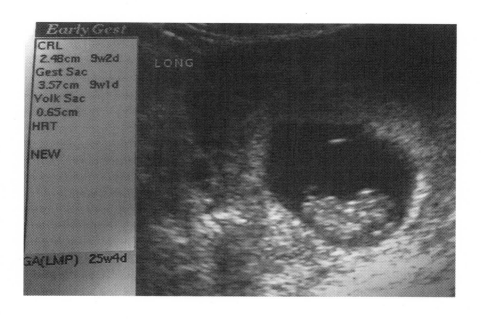

BEATEN

Unfortunately, I went to the doctor, and it was confirmed that I was pregnant. I was pondering what I was going to do now and reaching no conclusion. I didn't want to tell anyone about this. As if it couldn't get any more humiliating, I was now carrying my abuser's child. Well, I was definitely going to have the baby and just figured it out. I was finally about a couple of weeks away from moving out of the dorms. I'd decided that I was going to have no choice but to tell my family and stay with them. I couldn't afford a baby and an apartment on my own. I could only imagine the judgment but knew that they would still be supportive. I was also really missing my younger brother and wanted to resume our bond. We were very close, but unfortunately, when the asshole became very abusive, I didn't want to subject him to that. I kept myself hidden from so many people whom I loved in fear of judgment and him possibly doing harm to them. Just as I was contemplating what I was going to do, I received a phone call in my dorm room. Would you believe who it was? Yes, it was him calling me! I couldn't believe that he would even have the nerve to call. Unfortunately for me, I was now carrying his child and didn't want to keep that from him. I had all intentions on not telling him and just aborting the baby, but it didn't feel right. He said he wanted to talk, and I agreed to it. I picked a diner that I knew would be crowded enough that he wouldn't try anything but decent enough for us to talk. I was really hesitant at first but felt like it was fate who led him to call me weeks before I was going to be gone completely from school. I hadn't told my family, or anyone for that matter, that I was pregnant. I really didn't want to raise a baby on my own.

I was still very fearful of him but believed in my heart that sharing the news of me being pregnant would change him for the better. He was always very nice up until he wasn't. I was hoping that his niceness would last at least throughout my pregnancy. We talked about having children, and he was always very good with them. I was really nervous to meet up with him, not to mention our last encounter led to me getting twenty-six stiches. I put my fears to the side and took the chance. We scheduled to meet up early in the morning around eight. I arrived about thirty minutes earlier, giving myself some time to relax and gather my thoughts. Oh my goodness, here he came just strolling in with no care in the world. He walked in with the biggest smile on his face as he leaned over to hug me. I pushed him away and asked him to just take a seat. I wanted to hear what he was going to say first before I decided if I was actually going to share the news or not. He was once again very sorry for what he did. "I've heard all that before, so I don't believe you," I said. "I do want to know how the fuck you brought drugs to my school, when you told me you had left that life behind you." He told me that he was only doing it so he could find a place to stay. He continued to say "You've seen how I've been looking for a job and know that with my record, it was hard. I needed the money, so what did you expect me to do? I really apologize for bringing those drugs to your school and never expected to stay. That's why I had them on me. Remember I was just coming to gather my things and leave?" He had an excuse for everything, and it all stupidly made sense to me.

"I really didn't want to take up any of your time and so happy you agreed to meet with me," he said. "I need a favor and wouldn't be here if it wasn't important." I was looking at him like "Are you fucking serious? What favor could you possibly expect from me? After all the trauma you put me through, what else could you possibly want from me?" He continued to ask, "Well, you know the drugs they caught me with? I told them that they were for personal use, and I need you to back up my story and tell them I was a user. I'm also going to need you to tell the prosecutor that you didn't want to press any charges. I'm looking at some serious time and really can't handle going back to jail." At this point, he swore to me that he would go to an anger management program and work on getting himself better. He told me that if they believed the drugs weren't his and that he was a user, they would send him to a drug program instead of prison. I told him that I definitely wasn't going to lie to the authorities, but I would think about dropping the charges. At this point, I asked him if he was on drugs as his behavior didn't make any sense to me. I never thought about it before, but it could be very possible that he was. The abuse would always come randomly and for no sensible reason at all. He became completely offended and asked if that was what I thought about him. Mind you, he never denied it. I said to him, "You beat me, humiliated me, and threaten to kill me if I try and leave, and you're actually offended if I think you're on drugs?"

Despite all he'd done to me, I still wanted to help him out. He was going to be the father of my child, and I was going to need help raising it. After I agreed to drop the charges, he became extremely happy. He said he would figure the other part out. He leaned over to give me a hug, and I began gagging. He said, "Damn, I didn't know I make you that sick." I ran to the bathroom to throw my brains out. Upon returning to the table, he asked me if I was OK. I began crying and told him that I was pregnant. He had this big look of happiness on his face. He began screaming with excitement that he was going to be a father. I told him that I was looking for a place to stay but couldn't afford it with a baby. He told me that I was going to come and live with him. He was still living with his grandmother. He had his own room upstairs but told me that they actually just finished the basement. The basement was fully equipped with a bedroom, living room, bathroom, and eating area. It didn't have a kitchen, he told me, but we would just have to go upstairs to cook. I hesitated and reminded him that she knew about the abuse. He said, "That was in the past, and especially now you're going to have my baby, I would never do anything to hurt my baby, and she knows that." I told him to give me some time to think about it, and he agreed.

I had about two weeks remaining before I was going to be fully moved out of the dorms. I knew that I wasn't ready to tell my family this and couldn't face the judgment and humiliation. I did want to spend more time with my brother, but I would probably just go visit him when the baby was born. This seemed like the best option for me. I called him the next day and agreed to moving in with him. I did have some conditions. My first condition was that we had to talk to his grandmother together so I could make sure she was OK with me moving in. My second condition was that he had to get a legit job. I didn't care if he was working at McDonald's at this point. I wanted my child to have a father who wasn't a criminal. My final condition was that he never put his hands on me during or after the baby was born. He was so very excited and swore to me that he would do everything in his power to prove to me that he had changed. I'd never heard him this happy before. It really gave me hope that having his baby would actually be the changing factor in our relationship.

It was officially time to move in, and we had gotten the approval from his grandmother. She had one condition that if she ever caught him putting his hands on me, I would have to leave for me and the baby's safety. She also advised him that if he wasn't ready to go to jail, to not do it in front of her because she would call the cops. It really made me feel a little bit safer to know that she was aware of what was going on and was just as against it as I was. He always appeared to have the utmost respect for his grandmother, and that led me to believe he would be less likely to hit me again. I was feeling kind of excited as this was going to be our own private little apartment. We had already picked out furniture that his grandmother helped with. We even decided to paint the bedroom my favorite color red. We made a project out of it, and I have to admit it was fun doing these things with him. We painted the room together and had so much fun doing that. It was actually feeling like a normal relationship again. I was praying that he would stay consistent and be on his best behavior.

He was definitely communicating more and became more attentive to my needs. I'd never seen him so caring to that capacity. He was always calling to check on me, went to all the doctor's appointments, and made sure I was eating properly. He even kept his word and got a real nine-to-five job. It wasn't much, but it was something legal, where they gave him a paycheck with his name on it. Things were really starting to look up. He was working, and I was able to resume doing overtime at my job. The doctor was able to give me something that helped with the nausea and fatigue. We were saving up every little penny we made. We didn't have to pay any rent as his grandmother told us she wanted every penny to go to the baby. I was making plans for when the baby was born for me to go back and finish my degree. By the time the baby was here, my family would already know. His grandmother offered to help with the baby, and I know my family would too. Yes, things were definitely looking up.

I was now about three months into the pregnancy, and it appeared that everything was going well. I had, however, lost all my sex drive and had no desire to even be kissed by him. I wasn't sure if that stemmed from the hate I had developed for him during the abuse or the baby. The first month or so, I wasn't really depriving him of sex. Even though it wasn't often, he was getting a little something. Now in my almost third month, I didn't want him to even touch me. He began to get agitated and demanded that I gave him sex. He threw in my face that he was being the best man he could be. He reminded me, "I got a job like you asked, I'm not putting my hands on you, and I'm helping out as much as I can to support you during your pregnancy. If I can't get no ass from you, I might as well get it from somewhere else." At this point, I told him that I really didn't care because he definitely wasn't getting it from me. I tried to explain it to him as best as I could without him getting offended, that the drive just wasn't there. Of course, it didn't work out that way. I did acknowledge that I see him trying and did appreciate that. He was really not trying to hear anything I was saying at this point. He was pissed and continued arguing with me. I begged him to stop and reminded him that me stressing wasn't good for the baby. He agreed and told me that he was going to get some fresh air and get a drink at this bar he normally visited. I was just happy that he was leaving so I could finally get a peace of mind.

Hours went by since he left, and for some strange reason, I was really starting to feel bad. I wanted to talk to him and really needed him to know how I see him for what he was trying to do. Although the drive wasn't there, I was willing to bend a little and try. It was pretty cold outside, so I wrapped up really good. It wasn't far, the most fifteen to twenty minutes, which was more than enough time for me to freeze to death just walking to my car. I was going to the bar and surprise him and bring him back home and try to lay it on him, enough to last him a good week. I hadn't seen that much anger in him in a while and didn't want to be the cause of it coming back. It was pretty dark out and close to midnight. I really had no business going out there that late but wanted the fresh air as well. I finally arrived at the bar and started getting a little anxious. I knew he was going to be so happy to see me, or at least I hoped he would be.

As I entered the bar, my heart dropped as I saw no sight of him. It was surprisingly pretty crowded to be this late. I sat down for a little bit, thinking that maybe he went to the bathroom or something. Forty-five minutes had now passed and no sign of him. He didn't have a car, so he would have to have walked home. If he did, I probably should have seen him on my drive over there. It could have been that he also caught a cab or got a ride home. Either way, he wasn't there, so I just knew that I missed him, and he was probably already home. To my surprise, when I reached home, he was not there. I was at this point very upset and wondering where he could possibly be. I knew I told him I didn't care if he got ass from somewhere else, but of course, I didn't mean that. It was just me talking out of anger. He better had a great excuse for not being home yet. I was falling in and out of sleep, trying hard to stay awake from when he got home. I wanted to know the exact time he got home. It was now three in the morning, and he came stumbling into the bedroom.

I lay quietly and pretended that I was sleeping. I felt him look over my shoulder to check if I was really sleeping. He began shaking me to wake me out of my sleep. I continued to act like I was still sleeping. I was really upset and knew that if I confronted him now, we would definitely be arguing. For whatever reason, he insisted on waking me up. He aggressively shook me on and off for about at least thirty minutes till I couldn't play it off anymore. I pushed his hands off me and asked him why he was waking me out of my sleep. He told me that he couldn't believe that I was sleeping and should have been up waiting for him. I looked at him and rolled my eyes and turned back around. He was asking me why I had an attitude with him. "If anything, I'm the one that should be pissed at you," he said. As he continued to disturb my fake sleep, I became more enraged. I asked him where he was. He told me, "I went to exactly where I told you I was going." "It's three in the morning," I said, "and you just now getting home. "Well, the bar closed at two thirty, so I stayed till it closed," he told me. I told him to stop lying and tell the truth about where he was at. He was confused and asked how I could possibly know if he was there or not. I ignored the question and attempted to resume back to my fake sleeping.

He just wouldn't leave me alone. I tried everything not to reveal how I knew he wasn't where he said he was, but he kept pushing me. I finally screamed out, "I know you weren't there because I went to go look for you! I stayed there for almost one hour, and you weren't there, so stop fucking lying!" He was shocked as to what I just told him and asked me to repeat myself. I said, "You heard what I said. Now leave me the fuck alone." It always seemed like I had to get to that level of abusive language. He didn't seem to respond too well to me nicely telling him to leave me alone. "Why the fuck were you out there so late in the streets anyway?" he asked. "You are putting my baby in danger like that. Didn't you tell me to go ahead and fuck somebody else? So why would you be out there looking for me?" I just shut down at this point and decided to no longer respond. He was really drunk, and the abuse was ten times worse if he had been drinking. He was asking the same questions over and over, making it impossible for me to close my eyes or ignore him.

I jumped out of the bed and began putting my clothes on and leave. Honestly, I had no idea where I was going but knew I needed some peace and quiet. As I attempted to walk out the door, he pushed me to the bed. "Where the fuck you think you going with my baby in your stomach," he said. "You disrespecting me out in these streets like this? What were you really doing out there?" he asked me. He insisted that he was there and didn't see me. Now I was confused because I know that I'm not crazy or blind. I began doubting myself thinking that maybe I went to the wrong bar. I asked him just to be sure what bar was he at again. Of course, he confirmed the bar that I went to, and he wasn't there. Now I saw that he was trying to play games and fuck with my head. I got back up and asked him to please let me leave. I told him that I needed air just like I let him get. He continued with the same line of questioning but now asking me to identify this sideman I now allegedly had. Could you believe that this motherfucker was actually trying to turn this around on me, clearly trying to deflect his guilt on to me? As he continued on insisting it was someone else, I just became mentally exhausted. I screamed out, "He's whoever the fuck you want him to be!"

This time I knew that I was walking out this door. If I had to scream my way out and wake up his grandmother, I didn't care. I told him to get out my way and assured him that this was the last time I was going to ask quietly. "So you trying to get us kicked out," he said. I was ignoring everything he was saying to me and tired of getting up for him to push me back on the bed. I started screaming at the top of my lungs. Next thing I know, I was back on the bed but this time with a mouth full of blood and clutching my belly. He hit me with a really strong upper- and lower-cut punch. I got up to look in the mirror and saw blood just pouring from my mouth. I began crying. He was trying to calm me down and rub my belly at the same time. I continued screaming at him now and calling him a fucking liar. "You promised that you would never hit me again, that this would never happen! What the fuck did you just do?" I couldn't believe he not only violated me but also his unborn child. As I was talking to him, he burst out in tears. "Oh shit, oh shit, oh shit, oh shit, what the fuck did I just do?" He was pacing back and forth in a panic. "I'm sorry. I really didn't mean to do that." He was screaming to himself, "What the fuck did I just do?"

As I got up to go to the bathroom, I saw what appeared to be a tooth on the floor. He was trying to stop me from looking in the mirror and continued to say how sorry he was and didn't mean it. I was trying to go to the bathroom, and he was really trying to restrain me from going. I stopped and picked the tooth off the floor. I then used my tongue to make sure that I still had all my teeth in my mouth. Once my tongue completed the swipe from left to right and now reaching the middle, I began crying uncontrollably. "No, no, no, no, no, no, please don't tell me you knocked my teeth out." I was enraged and made my way to the bathroom, but this time, now realizing I figured out what happened, he didn't stop me. I looked in the mirror and opened my mouth, and my two front teeth were gone. I was lost and couldn't think straight. I ran back to the room and started looking for the other tooth. He kept saying sorry, and I told him to just find my fucking tooth. We searched for a good twenty minutes and no luck. There was blood everywhere it looked like a crime scene. My nightgown was full of blood. My face had all this dry blood, my hair had dried-up blood, my gums just kept bleeding, and my belly was in excruciating pain. I needed to go the emergency room and picked up the phone to call the police. He snatched the phone out my hands and begged me not to call the police. I told him that I needed the ambulance, I couldn't drive myself, and he didn't have a fucking driver's license, so how was I going to get there? He grabbed my hand and said, "Let's go. Please just let me take you. By the time they reach, I could have you there already."

Reluctantly, I changed my bloody clothes and allowed him to drive me to the ER. I remember pulling up to the ER and running out the car toward the entrance. My mouth was still bleeding, and I could barely stand. He quickly parked the car and ran in after me. As soon as I got the attention of the nurse at the front, she immediately ran over to me and asked what happened. On our drive to the hospital, he had already begged me not to tell on him. He said if they asked just to tell them that I had got robbed. He appeared so distraught, and I blamed myself for getting him to that point of anger (because he was doing so well until I denied him the sex). I agreed to go along with his story and told the nurse that exact story. She immediately took me to the back, and as we were headed to the back, he was holding my hand. She immediately stopped him and told him he had to wait outside. She boldly asked him, "Did you do this to her?" We both looked at each other with shock and said no at the same time. She said, "For your sake, I hope not," and told him to wait in the waiting area. As I was on the bed and she was guiding me to a room, she repeated the question. She said, "Sweetheart, did he do this to you? Please tell us now. You'll be protected here." I told her no and insisted that I got robbed. She asked me if I called the cops already to make a report. Of course, I told her a lie so she could leave me alone. As she left the room and I was awaiting for the doctor, she said, "At any time you want to tell us what happened, we won't judge you. We are here to help you." No matter how convincing I thought I was, she never believed me.

The doctor finally arrived into the room and asked me how I was doing. I told him that I was also pregnant and concerned about the baby. The doctor did all the assessments and asked all the questions to see how I was feeling and if the baby was in any immediate danger. I was asked if I had my teeth that were knocked out with me. The doctor said if I still had the teeth with me, they would have been able to insert them right back into my gums, but because I only had the one, it wouldn't have been successful. I was rushed to another room, where they did ultrasound of my belly to make sure that the baby was OK, and I had no internal bleeding. Once they did an assessment of the baby, I was returned back to the other room to finish the consultation of my teeth. I was told to follow up with my doctor, but as far as they could tell, the baby was OK. I was advised that it was too late to put the teeth back in my mouth because I needed both. They took an indentation of my teeth and gave me the option of getting some flippers in my two front teeth. I was told that I was pretty lucky that it was the two front teeth. It was easier for them to create flippers. However, it would take about six months for them to arrive.

My beautiful smile is gone forever. What he had taken away from me was irreversible, and I wouldn't be able to ever get that back. I wasn't sure about how I was feeling about now carrying this baby. Honestly, I had no emotions when they said the baby was fine. I just now saw myself being attached to this monster for the rest of my life. How was I going to go to work with no teeth in my mouth? The humiliation was just getting far from unbelievable. I already took time off from the last assault. Now what was I going to tell them this time? There was no way I could walk around with no teeth in my mouth. I was in public view where everyone could see me. Thousands of people would have to see me like this. I was instructed to stay overnight at the hospital just for the safety of the baby. They wanted to monitor the baby closely. The nurse also wanted me to stay as she was giving me chances to recant my story, but I never did. I slept in the dark alone once again feeling like my life was over. There was no way I'd be able to avoid my family for six months. I felt like I just wanted to die. I clearly didn't love myself. Abuse after abuse and I stayed. Even after this being the worse assault by far, I was still making excuses for him and blaming myself. I definitely saw no way out as I was still pregnant with his child and hiding from my family.

The following morning, he came to pick me up from the hospital. He had the biggest concern look on his face as if he knew that I could still at any given moment turn him in. He knew what he did was the next level of fucked up. To actually see myself with no blood running down my mouth and clear visual that I was toothless. I couldn't even smile, nor could I barely talk as the pain was unbearable. He picked up my pain medicine and catered to me for a little. I had to, of course, call out from work and contemplating if I would ever return. I knew they weren't going to give me six months off from work. Just as I reached home, I went straight to the bed and put the covers over me. I wanted to be invisible to the world and dared him to bother me. He knew he took something major away from me and had no choice but to feel sorry for me. I looked like a pregnant, missing teeth crack addict. I was done with the world and dared not face them. I stayed in my bed for about one week, not even showering. I couldn't bear to look in the mirror as every stare led to painful tears. Just as I felt like I could shut the outside world for a little, there was a knock on the bedroom door. It was his grandmother telling me my sister was on the phone. We had our own phone line, but my sister only knew her number. I still never told her that I was living there, and as far as she knew, I was still in school. Why was she calling the house? How did she even know that I would be there?

Grandma didn't know the level of deception I had committed with my family, so of course, she was going to tell her I was here and passed the phone. I reluctantly said hello, and all I heard on the other end was, "What the fuck are you doing there?" May I inform you that's major because my twin sister barely curses. So with that being said, I knew I was in for it. I tried to gather my lies together and see which one would sound better, but she didn't give me much time. I told her I was just visiting, and she told me bullshit. She had already called the school and spoke to my girlfriend who was still on campus. My girlfriend, of course, out of concern, spilled the whole tea. She told my sister about the assault on campus and that I withdrew from school. My sister had questions upon questions that I wasn't ready to answer. She told me that she was about to hang up the phone and come up there now, and I begged her not to. "Why can't I see you?" she asked. "I'm coming up there and don't care what you say." I told her that I just got mugged the night before and got assaulted really bad. I begged her to just let me get some rest and I'd reach out to her in a couple of days. I didn't tell her the extent of my injuries as she would have probably come that day. It was only a matter of time before she popped up. I knew that I couldn't avoid her much longer. I dreaded her seeing me like this, but there was no way for me to hide missing my two front teeth.

A couple of days went by, and of course, I avoided my sister like the plague. I had no intentions of calling her or seeing her for that matter. I was going to try and avoid her at least for six months. I didn't know how I was going to do it, but it didn't hurt to try. My sister, younger brother, and I were really close, and if it wasn't for this relationship, I would have definitely not been apart from them. I always felt like the less they knew, the better it would be for all of us. I didn't want them to stress over me, and I didn't want him thinking I was in contact with them that much. I wanted them far from his mind as possible. I was always scared that he would try and hurt them if I ever left him and went home. Needless to say, my sister wasn't having it. I was heading to the store so I could go get some more pain meds, and just as I was getting ready to pull off, there she was running toward my car. She looked into the window of my car and tapped on it for me to roll it down. I was so shocked to see her I didn't even have the common sense to roll the window down without being told. She looked into the car and just opened it and sat down. She was really happy to see me and began asking questions. I was barely talking, and when I did talk, I looked away as much as possible.

"Oh my god! What happened to you!" she screamed. "Where's your teeth? Who did this to you?" She began crying unconsolably, and I was trying to comfort her. I told her that was what happened when I got robbed. She became enraged and told me that she knew that he did this. "Where the fuck is that punk? I know he did this. Please let's just get your things and go. You don't have to be here. You're not safe. I know he did this to you. What, do you want him to kill you next?" "He's not going to kill me," I said, laughing it off. "I'm OK. You really don't have to worry." I really got robbed, I insisted, and even began telling her the elaborate story of how it happened. I told her I was outside pretty late looking for him, and these two guys came out of nowhere and took my money. I tried to fight them off, and that was when they punched me in the mouth and stomach. "Oh really," she said, "so what did they steal from you?" she asked unconvincingly. I told her they took my purse and money. "Which purse did they take," she asked. "How many purses do you have?" She knew I only had the one at the time. She reached to the back of the car and said, "You mean this purse right here with all your IDs, credit cards, and money still in it?" She asked, "What happened? They felt bad for you and bought it back to you?" I couldn't help but burst out with laughter. She said, "You might be fooling everybody else, but you not fooling me."

She stormed out the car and started making her way toward the house. I stormed out the door after her to stop her in her tracks. I jumped in front of her and asked her where she was going. She told me she was going to pack my bags for me since I couldn't do it myself. I hadn't seen my sister for at least five months. She finally stopped to look at me and said, "Oh my goodness, look at you. He's got you up in here with no teeth, just getting fat. That's exactly what he wants so he can have you all to his self." I told her that I was getting fat for a reason. She said, "Please don't tell me you stupid enough to be pregnant. How long did you think you was going to hide from me? Why would you keep that from me?" "You just literally called me stupid for telling you I'm pregnant, so you really have to guess on why I kept it from you." "Oh my gosh, have you lost your mind," she said. "We have to get you out of here. If you're pregnant, you nor the baby is safe." She was so visibly upset as she tried so hard not to look at me with the tears in her eyes. I begged her not to go inside the house. "He's there," I said, "and if he sees you trying to take my things, it's going to cause problems. I'm not leaving. This is where I need to be. Please respect that." It took hours for me to convince her not to go inside. She said, "I can't make you do nothing you don't want to do now, but if I have any suspicion that he touches you again, I will drag you out the house myself." She reluctantly left and started walking back home. I offered to give her a ride, even though it was literally right around the corner. She declined and said she needed to clear her head.

The following morning, there was a ring at the door. It was unusually early, and I went to answer it. As I opened the door, I saw my favorite cousin at the door. I was shocked because I hadn't seen her in quite some time and didn't even know she knew where I lived. "What are you doing here?" I asked. I gave her a hug and was so happy to see her. She hugged me and started crying. His grandmother came to the door and asked if everything was OK as she heard the cries. I introduced her to my cousin, and my cousin responded, "No, everything is not OK, ma'am. Do you see that she's missing two teeth?" His grandmother said, "I know it's so horrible that anyone would rob then beat up an innocent woman." My cousin looked at me and said, "Is that what she thinks happened?" His grandmother looked at me in shock and said, "Did he do this to you?" Now she started screaming out his name for him to come to the door. My heart was beating so fast. I couldn't believe this was happening right in front of my eyes like this. "How did you know I lived here?" She said, "That doesn't matter right now. You're getting your things, and you're leaving with me now." It then dawned on me that it was my sister who called her and told her what happened. My cousin was older and wiser. We looked up to her and always listened to her guidance. I guess my sister took a chance, hoping that I would listen to her.

Too many voices, everyone was talking at the same time. His grandmother was pissed as this was her condition, for no abuse to happen in her house. My cousin was busy telling me to get my things and go. He finally got to the door as we all were gathered at the front entrance of the door. He said good morning to everyone and asked what all the noise was. I went to introduce him to my cousin, and she said, "I don't want to meet him. I didn't come here for that. Get your things, and let's go." He was looking at me with anger and disappointment. "What's your problem?" he asked her. His grandmother started screaming at him. "Did you hit her? Are you the one that knocked her teeth out, and all this time you lied and told me she got robbed?" I gave my cousin a hug and asked her to kindly leave. I told her that was not what happened, and my sister just automatically assumed it was him because he had hit me in the past. She stared and looked directly at him and said no real man should be putting his hands on a woman at all. Both my boyfriend and I began insisting that everyone had this all wrong. He grabbed my hand and said, "Come on, babe, let's go." I walked away without even looking back at my cousin. She left and came back five minutes later with my uncle. Now I was completely embarrassed because he now knew my deepest, darkest secret.

I walked back to the front of the door, and my uncle had his arms wide open. I walked over and gave him a big hug. He said, "Sweetheart, do me a favor. Get as much stuff as you can get right now, and let's go." I politely told him that I wasn't leaving. My cousin standing right next to him said, "Well, I guess we not leaving either." My uncle said, "I really don't want to be here and hate that I had to get involved. Just get your things, and we will talk about everything else later." His grandmother came back to the door and said, "Well, who is this now?" She said, "This is too much drama going on in my house." She said, "Sweetheart, you got to go. Please get what you can and go." She said, "If he did this to you, you don't need to be with him. I told you guys I didn't want none of this bullshit in my house." She called him to the door and said, "She's got to go, and you not going to stop her." I didn't want any more arguing and didn't want to disobey my uncle. I felt horrible that he was involved and knew that they weren't going to leave without me. My boyfriend started fussing and saying that people just needed to mind their business. "She already told you guys she wasn't going." He looked at me and said, "You don't have to go if you don't want to. You're an adult, and you can make your own decision. You have my baby in your stomach. I need you close so I can make sure you guys are OK." In my head, I said, "Now you give a fuck. After you punched my stomach with the baby, you're so concerned about in me." I walked to our bedroom to gather as much as I could get. He followed behind me, and my cousin followed as well. I asked her to just let us talk and that she could wait outside the door. I told him I needed to go to clear my head and that my family could take a little better care of me. I told him that I would still come and visit and that we could go to the doctor's appointments together. He agreed and just lay back in the bed as I packed the remainder of my things.

I was so thankful that they came when they did. I really didn't want to be there. I was still having so much pain from mouth and my stomach. Each pain was a reminder that he did that to me. I had about three bags of clothes and shoes. My uncle grabbed two and my cousin one. They walked me to my car and followed me home. My sister was outside the door waiting for me as she knew the exact time I was coming. Thankfully it was pretty early, and my parents weren't home. I was able to put my things away and get situated. I didn't have to walk into them and having to immediately explain what happened to my teeth and that I was pregnant. I didn't want to face that disappointment immediately. My cousin and uncle stayed just a little to make sure my things were put away, and I was situated. They never asked any additional questions, just told me that they loved me and please take care of myself. My sister was so thankful to my cousin. She said, "I'll call you again if she acts up." My cousin said, "Please do. If I have to drag her out one hundred times, that's what I'll do." I asked my sister to please not tell our parents that he did this to me and stick with the robbery story. She said I could do that as long as I told her what really happened. I finally decided to tell her the truth. She agreed to prepare them with all the details of what happened to me so they wouldn't be too shocked when they saw me.

My family were very nosy went it comes to our immediate family, but surprisingly, they didn't ask to many questions. For my parents to have been as strict as they were when we were growing up, I was shocked at the level of privacy they gave me. I hadn't seen my parents in about the same time I hadn't seen my sister or brother. My parents were very disappointed that I was pregnant and didn't like my boyfriend. They knew nothing about the abuse but knew that he wasn't going to school or furthering his education. They were very keen on being with someone who shared the same ambitions as me. My younger brother was so happy that I was home but so sad to see that I was missing my teeth. He tried so hard not to stare, but it was hard not to. It really made being home so much easier. All the judgment I thought I was going to experience, I didn't. They were so hurt by the pain I went through with the alleged robbery they just wanted to make sure I was OK. However, they did express the need for me to go back to school.

Finally, being home really started to make me see things differently. There was so much peace and love. I didn't have to worry about anyone beating the shit out of me or possibly losing another part of my body. I was happy and had no desire to go and see him. I needed as much rest as I could get. I was physically and mentally exhausted. I really wanted to be free of him and felt this was finally my chance. Then the sharp pain in my belly reminded me that I was going to be attached to him for life. He called the house constantly, but of course, if my sister picked up, she would hang up on him. She never told me that he called either. I wasn't focused on calling him; I just wanted to focus on my future and the baby. I was also going to have to go back to work soon and face the world. I needed to practice how I was going to hide my missing teeth. I would practice covering my mouth when I talked. I told myself that I would also just talk less at work. I mean, that wasn't really hard. I was normally pretty quiet to begin with. If anyone did notice, I already had my lie ready for them.

Days went by, and I was really adjusting to being home. I was picking my brother up from school, we were spending much needed time together, and I got to see my sister when she got home from school and work. Aside from him calling the house every day, I was starting to forget he existed. The time spent with my family was unimaginably happy for me. We didn't do much, just ate dinner together, occasionally watched TV, and played games. His family dynamic was different from mine. He was motherless and fatherless. He had siblings, but they rarely spent any time together. They got along, but they didn't seem to be as close I would have expected for living under the same roof. His grandmother had to be both mother and father. I can only imagine how hard it was raising a drug dealer/women beater. He didn't understand what peace and love was. He was always so used to the streets. He would seem to try, but it was always so easy for him to revert to the negative. I should have known that me being here would anger him more. He knew that I would probably not want to come back, especially how we left off. Ignoring his phone calls only made him crazier and angrier than he already was.

We had had a long day, and everyone was getting ready for bed. There was a loud knock at the door, followed by back-to-back rings of the doorbell. I ran to the door with the suspicion of knowing it might be him. Once I got to the door, he was upset. "I've been calling you for almost one week now. Why haven't you answered my phone calls?" I told him that I was adjusted to being without him and really preferred it that way. I told him that my stomach was hurting every day, and my mouth was still in pain. Did you forget what the fuck you did to me? He began to get loud, and I asked him to leave. Of course, he insisted on not leaving, and I told him I would call the cops on him. He dared me to call the cops and said, "See what happens to your family's house when I get out. They can't keep you in there forever." Terrified by those threats, I pushed him away from the door and started to walk away from the house. We only got about two houses down, and my sister came running out the house. I swear this sweet, shy young lady was a beast when it came to confront my boyfriend. You would never believe that she would have that kind of courage or utter such foul words. She had no fear when it came to him. My fear started to grow more when he would make threats of harming my family, but if it wasn't for that, it would have been a little easier for me to leave and not look back. I really felt like I was there until I got pregnant with his child.

We were all the way to the top of the corner in front of the Chinese restaurant. Remember I told you we were getting ready for bed, so it was pretty late and quiet out. It was a weekday, and for the most part, everyone was probably in their beds also. I heard my sister's usually soft voice telling me to get in the house cause it was late. I told her to just let me talk to him for a little bit or he wouldn't stop calling the house. He told her to mind her business and get back in the house. She told him that she wasn't talking to him, so he shouldn't talk to her. He continued to tell her to mind her fucking business. My sister forcefully walked toward him and got right in his face. She dared him to make her go back in the house. "I want to see you make me get back in the house, you fucking punk. You can hit her cause she lets you. You not

BEATEN

115

going try that shit with me, you punk motherfucker. I'll call the cops with no hesitation and send your bitch ass back to jail." I couldn't believe she was in his face like that and had not wavered at all. She was so close that her spit was flying in his face. He backed away from her laughing and told her to get out of his face. Each step he took backward, she took the same step toward him. My sister was so disrespectful I just knew he was going to hit her. I was getting myself ready and seeing what I could grab to hit him with. It was crazy because I knew that if he hit my sister, I would beat the shit out of him. I don't know why I didn't have that same energy for myself. We were so loud in the streets I was surprised no one called the cops. She grabbed my arm and pulled me away from him. He said, "Don't worry, she'll be back. She always comes back." I turned around and said, "Not this time." He said, "You don't have a choice. You got my fucking baby in your stomach. I got you for life. You definitely not going anywhere now." The entire time I was walking back to the house, all I kept thinking was, *Wow, he does get me for life.*

I was about four months into the pregnancy and barely two weeks since the attack happened. I'd been having lots of complications with the pregnancy since that blow to the stomach. They said that the ultrasound looked fine, but it sure didn't feel like it. The pain was becoming a little too much to bear. One would think that at this juncture in life, you would be happy. I've always wanted children and imagined them being brought up in a loving environment. I was in my thoughts as the sunlight hit my face, hearing the sounds of birds chirping and footsteps back and forth as everyone was getting for either school or work. I wanted to wake up to happy thoughts, but they were just not there. Everyone looked in to check if I was OK, and off they went to the real world. I kept my pain silent, feeling like it would soon subside. The house was empty, and here it was, I was walking toward the bathroom and fearful of what lurked inside. The mirror force me to take a hard look of the peace I would never have. The once beautiful smile that had been taken away from me forever. Two missing front teeth that I would have to be without until another six months. Well, a little under six months, and the doctor did say there was a possibility they could come sooner. The stress of having to go to work and having my truth questioned each time. The truth that I would, of course, have to lie about. Being questioned alone of what happened would be a constant reminder.

Oh no, what a painful blow to the belly that was. I was surprised the baby didn't pop out right at that moment. Here it came again, another one of those sharp pains, so painful that it had bought me to my knees. I dreaded going out, especially to the hospitals. Since that encounter with the monster and my sister, I hadn't been able to sleep properly. Well, honestly, I hadn't slept in about two years. Yes, would you believe that it had been such a long journey in really hoping that this man would change? Twenty-six stiches later, two teeth knocked, I lost count of how many black eyes, bloody noses, and what was starting to feel like a monster made abortion, I was still here. Despite the taunting words of him being in my life forever, I really wanted the baby to be OK. I couldn't help but question what kind of father he would be to our child. He did punch me while the baby was in my stomach. Would he ever hurt our child the same way he was destroying me? I often wondered that. Oh no, another blow to the stomach, bringing me right back to my knees. This one was really bad; I think I might have to call him to take me to the hospital. On second thought, I would pass. Just started taking deep breaths and contemplating if I was going to drive myself to the hospital.

The pain is subsiding just enough for me to get myself to the hospital. The hospital thankfully was not even about ten minutes from the house. I got myself together and grabbed my pocketbook and car keys. As I was walking toward my car, I just saw shattered glass everywhere. Every single one of my car windows was busted, and when I say all of them, I mean all of them, not one left untouched. I looked around to see if the perpetrator was still here. Of course, we all know who the fuck did this. You have to be one low-life piece of shit to bust out the windows of the car of your future child's mother. We barely had any money as it was. He wasn't helping me with absolutely nothing. Pretty horrible that you just busted out my windows, now who was going to have to pay for them? That was money taken away from the welfare and care for your child. I just looked up to the sky and asked God to just put me out of my misery. This guy had taken everything away from me, and even after taking my teeth, he still wanted to see me suffer. I really thought this was it, that this last one would have softened him up. I ran back in the house and just started screaming. The added stress had now brought the pain back to a ten. I ran to the bathroom as felt like I had to pee. As soon as I pulled my pants down, they were already soaked with water. Then a burst of blood just came everywhere from my insides. It felt like I was a huge fountain as it just wouldn't stop. Blood everywhere! I fell to the floor and passed out. I just remember waking up in the hospital bed with my sister right by my side.

The following day, I didn't really know how to feel. It was a bit of grief with a sense of relief. I was no longer tied to this monster. My poor baby would have probably suffered more in the world. It felt like a divine intervention. Well, at least that was how I needed to see it to get me through the pain and grief. Everyone did tell me that maybe it wasn't meant for you to be attached to this guy forever. God had given me an out. Now it was up to you if you take it. He called me the next day to taunt me and ask me about my car. "How's your car doing?" he asked. "Why are you asking about my car? It's fine." I was playing it off like nothing happened. He sounded surprised at my response and told me, "Who's going to come over to check on the baby?" I told him to stay the fuck away from as we were no longer tied together by a baby. "You got what you wanted," I said. "The night you punched me in my stomach knowing that the baby was in there, what were you aiming to do? Why my stomach of all places? Then you damaged my car when I needed to go to the hospital. Did you not know that busting my car windows and leaving me with no transportation would have been damaging to me, leading the stress to harm our baby?" He began sobbing on the other end, insisting that I was lying to him. He had the nerve to ask me, "What did I do to our baby? I'm coming to see you." "No, the fuck you're not. You're going to stay the fuck away from me and my family. You can threaten to do whatever, but I won't hesitate to call the cops on you, and that's a promise."

3, D.   ... or 24 hours

IF TAKING ORAL PAIN MEDICATION:
1. Do NOT take on an empty stomach
2. Do NOT drive or drink alcohol

LIMIT ACTIVITIES FOR 24 HOURS
Special Instructions

Observe and Report the following:
Excessive swelling and redness, excessive bleeding occurring on dressing, extreme pain, pus drainage and temperature 100°F or above.

If you have any problems or questions, please contact your doctor immediately or hospital Page Operator: 972-6000, request to speak with the _____ Resident on call.
If unable to reach your physician with an urgent or severe problem, call the Emergency Room at 972-5123, or go to the nearest Emergency Room.

Prescription given: ☑ YES ☐

_____

Follow-up appointment _____

OTHER INSTRUCTIONS: No douches, no tampons, no xx, no baths x 2 wks. Take Tylenol only for cramps. Advil/Motrin + aspirin will increase bleeding

I have read and discussed the above instructions with the nurse/doctor and I understand them.

CHAPTER 13

SCARED STRAIGHT

I T WAS TIME to face reality and head back to work. I had already practiced how I was going to attempt to hide this no teeth business. My first day back and I was talking as less as possible. Of course, they would choose to talk to me more now that I was teethless as opposed to when I had teeth in my mouth. Either way, I had to toughen up. I had no choice. The first person to notice was my manager. She was heaven-sent and told me that I had nothing to be ashamed about. She was kind enough to put me in a post that I didn't have to talk to many people and would be away from passengers. I was so thankful as it just made life for me that much tolerable. By now, almost everyone at work knew that I got robbed and assaulted. Surprisingly, they were very considerate and really felt horrible for me. They would just mainly ask if they caught the guys who did it and how long it was going to be before I got my new teeth. I was so thankful that it wasn't as bad as I anticipated it would be.

The job was going really well, and now months in and I'd adjusted on not having teeth in my mouth. I'd mastered talking in a way where some didn't even notice that they were gone. I was starting to feel a little good about myself, especially knowing that I would have them back soon. I started picking up more hours as the overtime was highly needed. I started making plans to go back to school in a year or so. I wanted to get my own place and was getting ready to apply for a job that would change my life. I was going to be making so much money, and I heard the overtime was a lot. I was saving enough money where I can afford to live on my own but didn't want to apply for this new job until I had my new teeth. They were going to be just temporary flippers until I figured out how to get them more permanent. My family was really supportive and tried to do so much not to push me away. I guess seeing the effects that their strict parenting had on my ability to share things with them softened my parents up a lot. My parents, however, still never knew that I was being abused but did know that my abuser had a very bad temper. They were aware that he was the one who broke my car windows. He was constantly coming to the house looking for me, and I just wanted to take that away from them. I didn't know what he was capable of.

Just as I thought that I was getting ready to take that craziness away from the house, I came home, and there were about two cop cars at the house. My heart was racing as I thought that he probably did something to my family. I walked into the house and saw several police officers standing at the entrance of the door. "What happened?" I asked, and my mother told me that he just came to the house looking for me. She told him to stop coming to the house and that I wasn't there. She said he put his hands on his hip as if he had a gun and told her that she couldn't stop him from coming. I was mortified but even more so when the cops said that if she didn't actually see the gun, there wasn't much they could do. They said his words didn't sound threatening but did advise us to call the cops immediately if he came. They walked around the house to make sure that he wasn't lurking in the backyard and left. He stopped calling for a while after that, but I knew that I had to leave before my biggest fear became reality.

I'd finally found a place that was about twenty minutes from my family and pretty affordable. I was going to be moving in as soon as possible. I was headed to go and pick some of my belongings from the house. I tried to do them as early as possible as I knew that he wasn't really an early riser. I literally just pulled off from my family's house and already about five blocks away from the house. I was at the light, and I saw a bicycle driving in between the cars. I thought I heard my name, but it was not that clear. I got to another light, and this one was taking longer than the previous one. I saw that same bicycle, but I couldn't make out who was on it. The person had a hood over their head. I t looked like the bicycle was coming toward my car. The light was getting ready to change again but not before the person on the bike had reached my car. Knocking on the window of my car, I looked over, and it was him. I couldn't believe he rode his bike amid traffic, six lights down, and finally catching up to me. It was hilarious and cute at the same time. I hadn't really seen him since the incident with my sister and hadn't talk to him since the baby. I pulled over to the side so we could talk. He seemed to be nonthreatening and just wanted to talk. After that crazy bike ride to catch up to me, that was the least I could do.

He saw all the things in my car and asked if I was moving. I told him that was none of his business. I asked him if he actually came to my family's house with a gun, and he began laughing. He said, "Is that what your mother told you?" I said, "Well, clearly that's who said, but how would you know unless you were there?" He began rubbing my belly and said, "I know what you did to our baby. I'm not going to let that go. You took something from me. Now I'm going to take something from you." "What are you talking about?" I asked. "If you are threatening anyone, it should be yourself. You're the reason why our baby isn't here anymore. You're not even man enough to admit that this is your fault. No one to blame but you, and yet you want to blame others. What a waste," I said and started heading back to my car. "Don't walk away from me," he said. "I promise you will regret it. Now tell me all about where we are moving to." I said, "No, the hell not. There's no way you're moving in with me." He said, "We can do this the easy way or the hard way. I don't want to hurt you or your family. I love you, and you haven't given us a real chance. We had a chance with this baby, and it was taken away. I'm hurting just like you." He said, "We need to get through this together."

In fear that if I didn't agree to his terms of living with me, he would harass my family. I'd already brought enough stress to them. They were the most important things in my life, and if something happened to them because of me, I wouldn't be able to live with myself. He had me follow him back to his house so he could put his bike away and got right into the car with me. We were headed to the apartment, and I told him that it would probably be too late for him to be added to the lease. Once we arrived, I had to go to the leasing office, and he followed me there. Unfortunately, to my dismay, the leasing manager said it wouldn't be a problem to add him on and just needed ID. My family had already helped me with the furnishing of the place, and plus with my saving and income tax, I was able to have the place looking really nice. It sucked that he was going to reap the benefits and now disturb my peace. I'd rather mine be disturbed than my family's. Fortunately for me, my family was too busy to come and visit. I did tell him, though, under any circumstances could they know that he was living here. We agreed that if ever they did come, he would definitely have to disappear.

It was now a couple of months into the new place, and things had been pretty quiet. As far as he told me, he still had that job and able to help out with the bills. He was still trying to have sex with me, and when I realized that it was pointless trying to fight him off seeing he had no problem just taking it, I made sure I went and immediately got on birth control. There was no way I could risk the chance of getting pregnant by this monster again. He became a plague that I couldn't get rid of. He was a disease that I didn't want to contaminate others with. We were cut off from the world. His amazing family that we had the pleasure of spending time with didn't want him around after witnessing the abuse. We couldn't go to his grandmother's and definitely not my family. I didn't have many friends whom I trusted aside from my girlfriend at school. Unfortunately, I wasn't there anymore and weren't in contact as much. He'd taken everything from me it felt like the only choice I had was to just go with whatever he wanted. I tried leaving, but my fate always ended right back with him. This just seemed like this was going to be my life, and I was just going to have to make the most of it.

We were actually doing normal things like watching movies together, going to movies, cooking together, going to the mall, and laughing a lot. I never thought that I could laugh again with him. It was shameful, too, at time knowing that he was the reason why I could never laugh the same again. Things that we never seemed to do that often in the past. In the midst of this normal occurrences of our tumultuous relationship, I got some great news. The hospital called and said that I would be able to get my teeth sooner than expected. They were coming sooner than expected. I was so beside myself I didn't know whether to jump for joy or cry of happiness. Well, I decided to do both. I was so excited to share the news with him. He was the closest thing I had to a friend. I shared the news with him, and he didn't appear to be as happy as me. Well, anyway, I was not going to let him steal my joy. I was told that I could come within the next couple of hours or tomorrow. I'd waited months to have teeth again there was no way I was going to wait until tomorrow. I immediately headed over to the hospital as he accompanied me. We got to the hospital, and the doctor put them in for me. I looked in the mirror and immediately started crying. It wasn't my same smile, but it was a smile. I didn't have to walk around with this big hole in my mouth.

I was feeling so confident, happy, and I couldn't stop smiling. We walked back to the car, and I was jumping for joy. I expected for him to share in the moment with me, especially him being the one to take it away. He was so unhappy I couldn't believe it. Not one ounce of happiness for me. As a matter of fact, he was the saddest I'd ever seen him in a long time. It pained me to know that he was happy with me staying the way that I was. He didn't share in my happiness because he couldn't. He wasn't happy for me and couldn't even fake it. Either way, he wasn't going to take away my shine. My mood had changed for the better, and he was reaping the benefits of it. I actually responded back during sex instead of just lying there. I was cooking more often and just in a joyous mood. I couldn't wait to show my family the me that was taken away was slightly back. I was even able to put in for that job earlier than I expected too. Life was looking up. I asked him why he looked so unhappy now that I had my teeth back. He said to me, "I'm happy for you, but you looked beautiful either way." I looked at him and just shook my head. How could I possibly look good with no teeth in my mouth. He said, "I just mean that I am happy for you."

I'd applied for the job and received an immediate response. It looked like they were looking for people to start immediately. I interviewed weeks after getting my new teeth and actually got the job. Training was going to start in one week, and thankfully for us, it was paid training. I already gave my other job my notice. It was a bittersweet moment as I was really going to miss my coworkers. Here it was, another thing to be happy for and celebrate. I shared the news with him, and you could tell there was no happiness there either. I said to him, "Wow, it looks like you just want me to fail in life. Everything that's going on happy in my life, I'm sharing with you. I'm trying to have some sort of happiness. Don't you want to be happy, or you love just beating me down physically and emotionally?" He grabbed my face and said, "Of course not, babe. I love you, and I need to do better. I'm going to do better." It seemed like my words got to him a little, and he actually felt bad for the asshole he was being.

The next day, I came home from work to the cutest pit bull in the house. I was terrified of dogs because during my younger years, I got attacked twice. One dog was pretty big and the other one pretty small. I was chased by the big one, and the little one actually wound up biting me in the leg. It wasn't nothing too piercing but enough for me to be scared of them. It was since then that I never trusted them. I wasn't expecting a surprise but definitely not this one. I told him that he knew that I was scared of dogs, so why did he get one? I thanked him but told him I didn't want it in our place. He picked the dog up and put it to my face. "Look at this cute little harmless baby," he said. "This could be our baby." He convinced me that all dogs weren't so bad and that this one could be trained. The dog was so cute and so hard to resist. We started spending all our time when we got home with the dog. It was amazing as I never thought that I could ever have that kind of relationship with any dog. It was our baby, and we were grooming it to be a friendly dog. I would walk, feed, talk, and play with the dog. I would actually look forward to coming home just so I could spend time with our baby. It was a feeling of happiness that I didn't expect from a dog, but nevertheless, I was happy. I had my new teeth, about to start training soon, a newfound relationship, and a new dog.

Training had now officially started, and so far, I was loving the job. I would come and tell him about all the new people that I was meeting and how nice they were. Unfortunately, now by this time, my car was having mechanical issues that was going to cost too much to fix. I had to get rid of it and resort to catching the bus. Fortunately for me, this really nice lady in my training class didn't live too far from me and would offer to pick me up and take me home. What a godsent she was because I really dreaded taking the bus. I just needed to get through this training and get this job so I could get a loan for a new car. So I knew not having a car was only temporary. The training was actually seeming to be more fun than work. The instructors were really funny, and the class just seemed to be one little family. If the nice lady couldn't take me home because she wasn't going straight home, there was always someone to offer to take me home. The majority of us seemed to live relatively close to one another. Well, one day the nice lady couldn't take me home, and one of the guys from my training class took me home.

I got home and ran upstairs to get something that the guy and I discussed that I was going to let him borrow. Just as I was handing it to him and he was driving away, my boyfriend walked up from walking the dog. "Who was that?" he asked. "I thought you told me it was a lady that was picking you up and bringing you home." I told him that it wasn't a big deal. The lady had something to do, and he offered, so I accepted. He told me that if the lady couldn't bring me home, I should take the bus home. "I'm not comfortable with no man I don't know bringing you home." I laughed at him and said, "If you took care of your license issue and got a car, you wouldn't have to worry about that." I told him, "If someone offers me a ride, I don't care who it is. I'm going to take it." He was pissed at my response but had no choice but to take it. He said to me, "You are getting kind of bold now that you got that teeth in your mouth." I immediately stayed quiet and dared not respond. I told him that if it was a big deal to him, I had no problem just catching the bus if the lady couldn't bring me home.

The training was about a one month training. We had in-class training and then on-the-job training. I was doing a lot of studying, and once I got home, I was pretty tired. I wasn't spending much time or attending to our baby like before. I knew once I finished the training and had an actual schedule, things would be better. I did start noticing that our dog wasn't responding to me like before. I would wake up, and the dog would be on my side of the bed chewing on my underwear, which I found to be so strange. How could he chew on my underwear and not his? I told him about what I witnessed, and he just laughed it off like it was nothing. This behavior and him responding to me different was making me less comfortable with him. It wasn't the same as before, and he was getting so big so fast. It was scary how big he was getting. He wasn't that cute little puppy I fell in love with the first time. I would tread very lightly around him now realizing that he was barely listening to me and would only listen to my boyfriend. I tried to ignore it as much as possible.

Well, on a good note, training was officially over, and I got the job. We were almost one month into the job, and it was going wonderful. Over time was crazy, and I was making at least 40 percent more than I was making at the other job. A couple of us from the training class wanted to go out and celebrate. I was excited as I hadn't been out in a while with different people enjoying myself. I reached home after work and told him that we were planning on going out the next for some drinks and celebrate our new jobs. A few of us had the same days off and would be able to stay out late. He asked me if guys were going to be there, specifically the guy who dropped me off. I said that was a stupid question. Of course, there was going to be guys there. He told me that I wasn't going to be able to go. I said why wouldn't I be. He said because I didn't have his permission. I just decided to ignore because I knew he wasn't going to stop me from going out.

The next day, we woke up, and he asked me if I was still planning on going out. I told him if he had to get ready for work. He said, "Oh OK, that's how you are playing it. Well, you're off today, right?" I said, "Yes, I am." He calmly went and showered and got ready for work. He asked me again before leaving out, "So are you going out or not?" I ignored him once again. Meanwhile, he had our dog on a leash, which was weird to have him on a leash in the house. He said, "I'm going to ask you one more time and suggest you answer." I decided to ignore him once again. I heard him say, "Get her, boy." Then the dog started growling and charging toward me. He pulled him back with the leash, and the dog was just standing there growling and salivating as if I was going to be his next meal. Scared straight out of my mind, I pissed myself. I told him to please stop doing that. I told him that I wasn't going to go anywhere anymore. He said, "It's too late now. I gave you two chances." I attempted to walk past what used to be our baby to go get a change of clothes, and he charged at me again. This time he let go of the leash.

I immediately ran into the bathroom and locked it shut. I heard the dog growling behind the door and heard the front door open and shut.

I was screaming at the top of my lungs for him to put the dog away so I could get out of the bathroom. There was no response, just complete silence. Meanwhile, the phone was in the bedroom, and there were no windows in the bathroom. I was deathly afraid to come out that bathroom. As it seemed, he was grooming him to turn him against me. I noticed the change but had no idea that he would have been able to turn him against me like that. Hours and hours and hours went by and no sign of him. Thankfully, the bathroom was right there and had drinking water. I was starving but dared not even attempting to step foot out of the bathroom. It was daytime, and now you could see the light that was shining from underneath the bathroom door was getting darker. I must have woken up and fell asleep so many times. I must have been in there for at least twelve to fifteen hours. It felt like a lifetime. Finally, I heard the front door open. I started screaming for him to put the dog away so I could get out the bathroom. He rushed to the bathroom door and opened it. He fell to the floor and picked me up. "I'm sorry, babe. I really didn't expect you to stay in the bathroom the whole time." At this point, I was hungry and weak and just needed food.

I woke up the next day and knew this could no longer be my fate. I couldn't go home. That was out of the question. I had met some really nice people at the job but didn't know them well enough. Unfortunately, I didn't have a choice. I was going to need to tell someone. I needed to lie low for a while. There was no way I was going back to that apartment with him and the dog there. I called the nice lady the next day and apologized for missing the outing. I told her what happened to me and asked if I could get a ride to a hotel I was going to stay in for a little while until I figured things out. I waited till he left for work, and I told him that he needed to take the dog with him. This time I locked myself in the bedroom after he left out with the phone. I told him that I would call animal control and the police. He wouldn't leave, so I called the police and told them what happened, and sure enough, they came knocking on the door. His dumb ass had no choice but to leave with the dog. The cops told me they couldn't keep him away for too long and that I needed to have a plan. The nice lady arrived just as the cops were leaving. She offered to let me stay with her for a couple of days. I didn't want to outstay my welcome, so I told her I had another friend who offered to let me stay with them.

For about three months, I had to put my pride aside and ask for help. I was fortunate enough to have some genuine people let me stay with them. Some were really nice, and some weren't too genuine. I had stayed with one guy whom I thought was my friend, and I really trusted. He let me stay on his couch. I really thought, wow, not all men are assholes until I woke up to my tits in his mouth. So disappointed to say the least. I still had all my things at that apartment but had nowhere to go with them. I couldn't go home and let them know that I had failed once again. Not even making it to a full six months on my own and I'd already failed. I was, however, able to secure a vehicle. It wasn't much but something way more reliable than the car I had before. I knew my life was in danger, and I at least needed some form of transportation. You had to see the evil in his eyes when he told the dog to attack. It was one of the scariest moments of my life, especially considering I was already scared of dogs to begin with. I finally decided to call my friend from school, who had already told me she didn't have a roommate and offered to let me hide out for as long as I needed.

I had gotten all my things from the apartment but unfortunately couldn't take any of the furniture. I had to go the leasing department and have them remove my name from the lease. At first, they told me they couldn't, and then I took my flippers out my mouth. I told them that man I lived with did this to me and was on the verge of killing me. I needed to be off this lease, so I wouldn't have no ties to him. I sobbed so hard that snot was coming out my nose. The leasing manager being a woman herself began to cry. She apologized and said, "I'm so sorry you're going through this." She drew up an agreement removing me from the lease. I thanked her as we hugged and parted ways. She asked if I still had anything left in the apartment. She offered to have the superior accompany me since I wasn't sure if he was home or not. I had a safe with all my important documents that I had completely forgotten about—my social security card, immigration papers, birth certificates, and much more. It wasn't there. The asshole removed it. Those were my very important papers, and I couldn't walk away from them or leave them in his hands.

I had a feeling that he would have stored them at his grandmother's. I had no choice but to go there and look. I called the house and told her that I had these important docs that I thought I might have left at her house. She sounded happy to hear from me and said, "Of course, you can come and take a look." I asked her if he was there, and she told me he hadn't been there for over six months. She said if he came around, it was mainly when she was at work, so she hadn't seen him. I timed it with just enough time for her to let me in the house as she was leaving out to run errands and visit family. As soon as I got into the basement on where we used to stay at, I knew exactly where to look. Unfortunately, it wasn't where I thought it would be, so I started looking around the entire house. They had a garage, but I didn't have the key. His younger brother happened to come home at the exact time I was giving up and opened the garage for me. There it was, my safe with all my important paperwork. I immediately grabbed it and went downstairs to grab some things that I noticed I left behind.

Just as I'd gathered all my things and headed out the door, he was standing right there. He pushed me back into the room and started smacking everything out my hands. He asked what I was doing in his house and said that I was trespassing. He said, "Did you not think that I would know you were here?" So I was assuming that his brother told him. I told him that his grandmother let me in, and technically, it wasn't because my license still had the address on it. I never changed it over as I dreaded those visits to the DMV. I told him to get out of my way and began having flashbacks of that dreadful moment he knocked my teeth out my mouth. I tried to push my way out, and he pushed me and slapped me so hard that my flippers fell out my mouth. Blood was coming from my mouth, and as soon as I tasted it, I became enraged. I start screaming and pushing him back with all the force I have in me. He stumbled to the ground, and I started kicking him. As I was kicking him, I was crying. I was asking him, "Haven't you had enough, motherfucker! What else do you want to take from me!" He grabbed my legs and pulled them from under me. I fell back to the bed; I then saw him going for my teeth. He grabbed them and ran to the bathroom. He threw them into the toilet bowl and flushed them down the toilet. At this point, all I saw was red. How could he be that evil? He already took them once, and now he wanted to take them again.

I ran back to the bedroom and grabbed a bat that was in his closet. I hit him right in his back so hard he fell to the floor. I hit him a couple more times in his legs and his hands. He was down enough where I could run to the bathroom and look in the toilet bowl. Such a big sigh of relief when I see that he didn't successfully flush them down the toilet. I immediately put my hands in the toilet bowl and grabbed them. I ran back to the bedroom so I could get the safe and leave. At this point, nothing else mattered. He came from behind and put his arms around my neck. He turned me over and put his knees in my stomach, and he had a death grip around my neck. I couldn't breathe and was fighting to get him to release the hold he had on my neck. I got the courage to wiggle my way out and kick him right in his balls. At this point, I had to leave everything behind and run for my life—the safe, my purse with my car keys in it, and my other belongings. My shirt was completely torn with nothing but my bra exposed. The shirt was covered with blood, and so was my face and hands. I got him really good that he was also bleeding.

On my way out the door, I was screaming for his brother to call the police, but apparently, he had already left back out. Before stepping foot out the door, I grabbed a big knife that was in the kitchen. I was prepared to stab him. At this point, it was either my life or his. I didn't care if I had to fucking kill him. That was what I was going to have to do. I finally got free and started screaming for help. This big black car stopped and started driving toward me. This man rolled his window down and started screaming, "Oh my god! What is going on, honey! Oh my god! What happened to you!" I cried, "Please help me. You have to get me to a police station." Not realizing that I still had the knife in my hand, he said, "Okay, but you got to get rid of that knife." I immediately jumped in the back of the car as he drove me to the police station. Just as we were pulling off, I saw him running out the house toward the car.

If it wasn't for that Good Samaritan, I have no doubt in my mind he was going to kill me. He had his hands on my neck so tight I felt my life leaving my body. We pulled up to the station, and I thanked the driver and ran. He said, "Young lady, please take care of yourself." Before he could pull of, the cops flagged him down, and he had to give details of what happened. All he could tell them was that he found me on the streets bloody and with a knife in my hand, asking for help.

I was in panic mode and told the cop that he just tried to kill me. I told them that he also had my new teeth after knocking out my real ones. I urged him to leave now before he left the house with my things. I knew that I would never see them again. I suffered too long with no teeth in my mouth I couldn't bare that humiliation again. The cop was enraged and saddened at the same time. We got into the car, and he was telling me, "You have to leave, or he's going to kill you." He said I'd been doing this for a long time. He told me, "I know this isn't his first time hitting you either." He said, "Did you say he knocked your teeth out? Leave, young lady. I promise you it only gets worse from here."

Just as we were pulling up to the house, there he was walking with the dog, my safe, and pocketbook and getting into my car. The cop pulled the car right in front of him and jumped out the car. I told the cop his name, and he asked, "Are you this guy?" Of course, he denied and said that he had no idea who I was. I wasn't sure how that was going to fly considering he had all my belongings and getting into my car. I jumped out the police car and said those were my bag, my safe, my car, and he had my teeth. As soon as I said that, the asshole started laughing. "You think this is a joke, you punk?" He had them put my things on the floor, and I grabbed everything. I took out my license and showed him that I once resided here. I showed him my insurance and everything. He said, "I don't need that. I know he's lying. He looks like a liar." He put him in handcuffs and put him in the back of the car. I begged the cop to make him tell where he put my teeth at. He insisted he had no idea what I was talking about. The cop grilled him for about thirty minutes, and he still wouldn't confess to having them or their whereabouts. I was at this point just sobbing on the floor. I couldn't go another moment without teeth in my mouth. He had them. I know he did. Thank goodness this cop decided to now check on his person. He had a pair of jeans that had so many individual little pockets. He said, "Is he a drug dealer, because that's usually what they wear to be able to store their drugs in different places?" After a twenty-minute search, he found them hidden in the smallest pocket I ever saw. I just fell to the ground and started crying. My life and humiliation were spared. If I went back to this asshole, I was as good as dead. The cop took my statement and then escorted me to the hospital to get looked at. He went off to jail, and I was thankful to still be alive with my teeth back.

CHAPTER 14

THE ESCAPE

H E'S SERVING TIME, I believe three to five years. I'm not going to lie, in the beginning of his sentence, he did reach out to me and pulled on the weak heartstrings I had for him. I visited him and wrote him for about one year. With all the things that he'd done, how could I still be attached to him from behind bars? It wasn't as easy as everyone may want to believe it should be. I was groomed from since the beginning to conform. He started out as one of the nicest guys I ever met and turned out to be one of the biggest monsters I knew. It really felt like he loved me in the beginning. He was the monster who loved me, at least I thought it was love. I wanted to believe he was sorry and didn't mean it, but each time it got worse. When I got the courage to leave him, he started threatening me, and when he saw that wasn't working anymore, he threatened my family. He became a drug that I was addicted to, and I needed help to break this addiction.

Thankfully for me, I found my escape from the prison I've been in for years. This guy was pursuing me about one year before he went to jail. After he got locked up, he pursued me even more. I finally broke down and gave him my number, and we talked. We began talking a lot. It was different times of the day and sometimes pretty late. He then asked me, "If you have a boyfriend, how are you so free to talk to me like this?" I felt comfortable enough to be honest with him and tell him that he was in prison. I told him about the assaults, drugs, and near-death experience. He said, "This man has about five years. You're beautiful and already wasted too much of your time to begin with. God has given you a way out, and you should take it. He can't come look for you or threaten your life. He's already been in jail and serving time for your assault. I'm pretty sure once he gets out, he's wanted to be as far away from you as possible." I decided to take a chance and move on with my life. We began dating, and I have to tell you it felt so good being with someone who didn't have to beat me. This man treated me so good that I didn't even know I could ever be treated this way.

I lacked self-esteem from since I was younger. It didn't help that those kids were so hurtful and teased us for most of our childhood. Things like that can honestly have such an impact on someone's life. It didn't help having my innocence violated by someone I trusted. I just wanted a chance at feeling loved and felt like he deserved to give it to me. That's why I gave him chance after chance just to realize that he didn't get better. A person can only do what you allow them to do to you. From that first time he hit me, and I stayed, I told him that was what I was willing to accept. Each time after that, I forgave him, so he knew that he could continue with the same pattern of behavior, and all he had to do was say he was sorry, and I would take him back. I'm here to tell you that it doesn't get better. They never change and only become emboldened by the first acceptance of that first blow.

I lost so many chances of being a better version of me. I turned away so many amazing men who could have possible been my future. I lost time with my family that I could never get back. I lost something that can never be replaced with the originals (my teeth). For so long, even with the replacements, I never fully smiled like I once did. I've lost so many friendships and pushed so many people away. I'm thankful for the young lady who stood up for me at his first display of public abuse. I'm thankful for those visiting the dorm who came to my rescue. I'm thankful for my dorm mate-turned-friend being a listening ear. I'm thankful that my sister was the amazing other part of me who had common sense to let others know what was going on with me. I'm thankful for all those who opened up their door for me and gave me safe and peaceful places to rest my head when I felt my life was in danger. I'm thankful for my uncle and cousin who were so bold enough to come to the house and attempt to rescue me. The worst thing I did in this situation was staying quiet and hiding it from my family. Till this date, most of my family and parents didn't find out until almost a decade after the attack.

I'm hoping that in reading this book, it can be the escape that you or a friend might need to break free. There are so many more resources available now that weren't available in the past. People do care, so don't push them away when they genuinely offer help. Sometimes they can be what's standing between you and a death sentence. Don't keep silent. At least let one person know what is going on. Never be scared to call the cops. Always know that it's not your fault. There's nothing that can make anyone who love you violate you by smacking, kicking, or punching you down. This goes for men too because it's not just women who get abused. You're not alone in this fight. So many didn't live to tell their story. I will forever be grateful to God that I lived to tell my story.

VICTIM'S IMPACT STATEMENT

THE STATE OF NEW JERSEY, VICTIMS AND SURVIVORS OF CRI
E NOW GIVEN AN OPPORTUNITY TO ADDRESS THE COUR
FENDANT HAS BEEN FOUND GUILTY OF A CRIME AND IS SCH
SENTENCED. THIS STATEMENT TO THE COURT IS CALLED
ACT STATEMENT. THE PURPOSE OF THIS STATEMENT IS
W THE CRIME PERPETRATED AGAINST YOU HAVE AFFECTED
BOTH YOU AND YOUR FAMILY. THE JUDGE THEN CONSI
UT AS A SIGNIFICANT FACTOR WHICH WILL ASSIS
TERMINING, A JUST SENTENCE TO IMPOSE UPON THE DEFEND

FILLING OUT A VICTIM'S IMPACT STATEMEN

- ANSWER THE FOLLOWING QUESTIONS TO THE   BEST OF YOUI

- IF YOU NEED ADDITIONAL SPACE, FEEL FREE TO ATTACH EXTRA

- SUBMIT YOUR WRITTEN STATEMENT TO THE OFFICE OF

  ADVOCACY <u>BEFORE</u> THE DEFENDANT IS TO BE SENTENCED.

  IF YOU WISH TO MAKE YOUR STATEMENT ORALLY BEFORE TH

  NOTIFY THE OFFICE OF VICTIM/WITNESS ADVOCACY.

RE INFORMATION OR ASSISTANCE IN PREPARING YOU
EASE CONTACT US. AFTER COMPLETING YOUR VICTIM
STATEMENT, PLEASE SEND OR BRING IT TO:

We are aware that you have been a victim and/or witness to a crime. Please be advised that in accordance with N.J.S.A. 52:4B-36, the Newark Victim/Witness Advocacy Program is here to assist victims and/or witnesses of crimes committed within the City of Newark by offering to you the following services:

(1) Direct referral to social service agencies (public and/or private)
(2) Information on case status
(3) Information on the Criminal Justice System
(4) Assistance in the return of property
(5) Assistance in filing a Victim Impact Statement
(6) Provide court accompaniment, when necessary and requested
(7) Assistance in filing applications with the NJ Victims of Crime Compensation Board
(8) Give support in a caring manner

We are enclosing at this time a Victim Impact Statement with instructions for completing same. Please complete and return the Statement as soon as possible. If you need assistance, in completing same please not do hesitate to contact us. If you should change your address and/or phone number, it extremely important that you inform us.

If additional information or assistance is needed, please do not hesitate to contact us at (973) 7__ 4862. Our services are offered to you free of charge.

We at the Newark Victim/Witness Advocacy Program of the City of Newark, Law Departm__ located within the Office of the Prosecutor, look forward to meeting with you.

Sincerely yours,

Printed in the United States
By Bookmasters